Deliberative Democracy and the Environment

Can our political institutions be more sensitive to environmental values? Why should greens be interested in deliberative democracy?

Contemporary democracies are frequently criticised for failing to respond adequately to environmental problems and our political institutions are often charged with misrepresenting environmental values in decision-making processes. In this innovative volume, Graham Smith argues that the enhancement and institutionalisation of democratic deliberation will improve reflection on the wide range of environmental values that citizens hold.

Drawing on theories of deliberative democracy, Smith argues that institutions need to be restructured in order to promote democratic dialogue and reflection on the plurality of environmental values.

Deliberative Democracy and the Environment makes an important contribution to our understanding of the relationship between democratic and green political theory. Drawing on evidence from Europe and the United States, it systematically engages with questions of institutional design. This book will be of interest to students and researchers in both environmental and democratic politics.

Graham Smith is a Senior Lecturer in Politics at the University of Southampton. He is the co-author of *Politics and the Environment* and has published a number of essays on democratic and green political theory.

Environmental Politics/Routledge Research in Environmental Politics
Edited by Matthew Paterson, Keele University, and Graham Smith, University of Southampton

Over recent years environmental politics has moved from a peripheral interest to a central concern within the discipline of politics. This series aims to reinforce this trend through the publication of books that investigate the nature of contemporary environmental politics and show the centrality of environmental politics to the study of politics per se. The series understands politics in a broad sense and books will focus on mainstream issues such as the policy process and new social movements as well as emerging areas such as cultural politics and political economy. Books in the series will analyse contemporary political practices with regards to the environment and/or explore possible future directions for the 'greening' of contemporary politics. The series will be of interest not only to academics and students working in the environmental field, but will also demand to be read within the broader discipline.

The series consists of two strands:

Environmental Politics addresses the needs of students and teachers, and the titles will be published in paperback and hardback. Titles include:

Global Warming and Global Politics
Matthew Paterson

Politics and the Environment
James Connelly and Graham Smith

International Relations Theory and Ecological Thought
Towards synthesis
Edited by Eric Lafferière and Peter Stoett

Planning Sustainability
Edited by Michael Kenny and James Meadowcroft

Deliberative Democracy and the Environment
Graham Smith

Routledge Research in Environmental Politics presents innovative new research intended for high-level specialist readership. These titles are published in hardback only and include:

Deliberative Democracy and the Environment

Graham Smith

LONDON AND NEW YORK

First published 2003
by Routledge
11 New Fetter Lane, London EC4P 4EE

Simultaneously published in the USA and Canada
by Routledge
29 West 35th Street, New York, NY 10001

Routledge is an imprint of the Taylor & Francis Group

© 2003 Graham Smith

Typeset in Sabon by
Prepress Projects Ltd, Perth, Scotland
Printed and bound in Great Britain by
T J International Ltd, Padstow, Cornwall

British Library Cataloguing in Publication Data
A catalogue record for this book is available from the British Library

Library of Congress Cataloging in Publication Data
Smith, Graham, 1966–
    Deliberative democracy and the environment / Graham Smith.
        p. cm.
    Includes biographical references and index.
    1. Green movement. 2. Democracy. 3. Environmental ethics.
    I. Title.

    JA75.8 S56 2003
    320.5 – dc21   2002151949

ISBN 0-415-30939-5
ISBN 0-415-30940-9 (pbk.)

To Susan

Contents

Acknowledgements

This book has been a long time coming. Other commitments meant that I was forced to work on the manuscript in stops and starts. However, this may have had a beneficial effect in that I was able to return to the text refreshed and with new ideas. The perceptive comments and suggestions of a number of colleagues certainly improved the book. Mattias Ask, John Barry, Chris Brown, James Connelly, Andrew Dobson, Marius de Geus, Raymond Plant, David Owen and Susan Stephenson all read and commented on at least one version of the text at some point over the last five years. I would like to thank them for being so generous with their time and energy. I have tried to respond to their suggestions, but, as ever, final responsibility for the book lies with me alone.

Other people have contributed in different ways. When I first arrived in Southampton I was fortunate to spend time in the company of a number of political theorists, in particular James Connelly, Jim Doyle, Liam O'Sullivan and Susan Stephenson. A better form of education and friendship could not be asked for. Sadly, Liam died last year, and he is greatly missed by all of us. I have benefited considerably from listening to and arguing with members of the community of green and democratic theorists. The early IRNES (Interdisciplinary Research Network on Environment and Society) conferences and more recent ECPR (European Consortium for Political Research) workshops have been particularly important to the development of my ideas and (more importantly) new friendships. I would also like to thank my other friends in Salisbury, Southampton, Edinburgh, Glasgow and elsewhere for taking my mind off the book and other work commitments.

Frank Cass kindly gave permission to reproduce sections of 'Taking Deliberation Seriously: Green Politics and Institutional

Design', originally published in *Environmental Politics*, and Blackwell Publishing gave permission to reproduce sections of 'Citizens' Juries and Deliberative Democracy', co-authored with Corinne Wales, which originally appeared in *Political Studies*.

Finally, I would like to express my deepest thanks and love to Susan Stephenson. Without her support and encouragement I would never have begun my doctoral studies, let alone finished this book. I dedicate this book to her and to our life together.

Graham Smith
Salisbury
October 2002

Introduction

In the last few decades of the twentieth century, environmental problems became a higher priority for governments, citizens and other bodies. Liberal democracies now have dedicated environmental ministries and agencies and an imposing array of environmental policies; governments are party to a seemingly impressive range of environmental agreements and regimes at the international level; citizens are generally more sympathetic towards the campaigns of environmental organisations. These developments have emerged in response to the recognition of the importance of environmental values, and yet there continue to be high levels of conflict around issues such as the release of genetically modified organisms, road building, the destruction of rainforests and climate change.

Value conflict is at the heart of environmental politics. Decisions that affect the environment are typically multi-faceted: when reasoning about the non-human world, individuals and groups often find themselves pulled in contradictory directions, appealing to values that they find difficult to reconcile. The central question that this book attempts to answer is how political decision-making processes might be structured so that they are sensitive to this plurality of environmental (and other) values.

The environmental movement itself can be understood as being born out of value conflict, a conflict with interests in society that did not recognise or give sufficient attention to environmental values. Greens have challenged the values associated with the idea of progress based on ever-increasing levels of economic growth on the grounds that it represents a failure to consider the full range of values that we associate with the environment.

But it is important to remember that the environmental movement itself is pluralistic in nature. So, for example, we find distinctions drawn between preservationists and conservationists, between ecologists and environmentalists, and between ecosocialists, social ecologists, ecofeminists, animal liberationists, bioregionalists, deep ecologists and advocates of environmental justice, to name but a few distinct positions. Different factions within the broad environmental movement draw on different conceptions of environmental values. The way in which different environmental and non-environmental values are prioritised at times places their proponents in conflict with one another. The classic example is the conflict that can emerge between conservationists and preservationists, 'often with that special degree of hostility reserved for former allies' (Passmore, 1980: 73). Conservationists are typically concerned with ensuring sustainable yields of environmental resources for on-going human consumption; the preservationist ethic, in contrast, argues for the protection of areas from direct human interference, often on the grounds that aspects of the non-human world have intrinsic value. Again, the 'special degree of hostility' has famously been witnessed between social and deep ecologists. Murray Bookchin, the founder of social ecology, frequently rails against the 'mysticism' that he sees as prevalent within deep ecological thought (Bookchin, 1987; 1991). As Kate Soper recognises: 'The ecology movement, when viewed as a whole, draws its force from a range of arguments whose ethical underpinnings are really quite divergent and difficult to reconcile' (Soper, 1995: 254).

If we take one of the most celebrated sites of environmental conflict – the world's rainforests – we can begin to appreciate the plurality of values associated with the non-human world. At an instrumental level, the rainforests have direct use for us in a number of ways. We value their role in climatic processes, acting as a carbon dioxide sink to secure basic ecological conditions for human existence and flourishing, and as a resource for timber, pharmaceutical and other products. Prudential appeals are frequently made to the scientific value of such unique ecosystems and the possible advancements in medical and scientific knowledge that could be gained from the study of the rich biodiversity. Using the language of justice, conflicting arguments have emerged about the rights of indigenous peoples to remain in the environment that has always provided the background for their form of life, and the rights of individual nations to self-determination in exploiting resources within their national territory. Appeals to justice have also focused on the rights of future generations, pulling judgements about the value of the rainforest in a different direction. Ethical considerations have been extended to the diversity of non-human entities that constitute the ecosystems of the rainforest. Not only is the very existence of such 'wild' places often constitutive of individuals' own sense of identity and understanding of the relation between human and non-human worlds, but their existence can be judged as significant in their own right. If we return to the classic distinction between conservationists and preservationists, for the former the value of the rainforest might lie in developing sustainable yields so that timber resources will be available to future generations; preservationists will tend to emphasise the value of wilderness untouched by humanity. Since the significance of the rainforest is dependent upon the relative weight given to these different types of values, we can begin to see how judgements about the environment pull us in different, and at times competing, directions.

John O'Neill has offered a number of instructive examples of value conflict (O'Neill, 1993: 108–9; 1997: 75–7). One will suffice here: the value of wetlands. The value of a wetland will change depending upon whether we focus attention on its landscape value or its species richness. Even if we are simply appealing to the value of species richness, conflict can emerge between ornithologists and botanists over policies towards drainage:

> Crudely speaking, from the ornithologists' perspective, the more water, the greater reed beds and open water, and hence more kinds and numbers of birds; such considerations might lead to a recommendation to cease current drainage patterns and allow an area to flood. However, from the botanist's perspective, some of the most interesting plant communities might sometimes be destroyed by that policy.
>
> (O'Neill, 1997: 75)

Nowhere is this clash and conflict of values more apparent than in the debates over the nature of sustainable development. For many, sustainable development is the core principle at the heart of green politics: the ground on which debates over humanity's relationship with the non-human world are progressing. Unpacking the concept, it becomes clear why conflict rages. A commitment to sustainable development not only requires reflection on values associated with environmental protection, but also raises questions of quality of life, social justice, intergenerational justice and democracy (Connelly and Smith, 2003). The concept of sustainable development reminds us that environmentalists are not concerned with only a narrow range of purely 'environmental' values. The relative weight given to environmental values in relation to other values such as justice is at the heart of debates. Different conceptions of sustainable development not only 'balance' or prioritise these values in different ways, but at times draw on different conceptions of the values themselves. Justice can be based on desert, merit or needs, and the obligations it generates may be seen as universal or as primarily related to particular moral communities. Policies may well differ depending upon the particular conception of social justice. Again, there is likely to be conflict between environmental protection policies based on a conservation ethic (the desire for sustainable yields) and those based on a preservation ethic (the independent moral worth of non-human nature). Decisions on particular policies may involve judgements in which obligations to current generations, future generations and non-human nature pull in competing directions (Dobson, 1998).

It is not surprising, then, that there are a variety of different conceptions of sustainable development, based on different interpretations and relative weightings of competing values. Ecological modernisation – at present the dominant conception of sustainable development – is a discourse of eco-efficiency. Its primary concern is the efficient use of natural resources within a capitalist framework (Hajer, 1995; Christoff, 1996a; Gouldson and Murphy, 1997). Criticisms have been levelled at the lack of attention paid to social justice (both within and between nations) and the failure to conceive of nature beyond its value as a resource. In contrast, models that promote the rights of Third World development will give relative priority to social justice: the redistribution of wealth becomes a precondition to sustainability. Again, the more radical vision of sustainable development as bioregionalism gives priority to environmental values, with little concern to the question of resource distribution across bioregions (Sale, 1985). Social justice is of secondary concern, as is democracy. The conception of sustainable development favoured will clearly have an impact on the type of policies to be pursued. At times policies may overlap; at other times they will conflict.

Contemporary polities are therefore faced with the problem of developing policies in the light of conflicts between a plurality of values, many of which relate to the relationship between humanity and non-human nature. Conflict occurs *within* and *between* individuals and *between* different elements within the environmental movement itself. This book attempts to understand the nature of the conflict between environmental (and other) values and how the plurality of environmental values might be accommodated within political decision-making processes.

The first task, then, is to consider the nature of environmental values. Chapter 1 begins by analysing two influential tendencies within environmental ethics: the belief that nature has intrinsic value and the search for an overarching (monistic) ethical theory to guide our interventions in the non-human world. In response to the attempt that these two tendencies make to 'overcome' value conflict, an alternative perspective – value pluralism – is offered that recognises that environmental (and other) values are often incompatible and incommensurable. The question then becomes 'How might we design institutions that are sympathetic to value pluralism?'

Chapter 2 focuses attention on how liberal democratic states have responded to environmental values in decision-making processes. One of the fundamental principles guiding decision making in liberal democratic institutions is the aggregation of individuals' preferences into a collective choice: thus the important roles played by voting and techniques such as opinion polling and cost–benefit analysis (CBA). It is the latter technique – CBA – that is much favoured in policy assessment. In recent years, environmental economists have promoted the extension of CBA to systematically incorporate environmental costs and benefits. Environmental economists appear to be sensitive to different aspects of environmental value and have developed innovative and sophisticated techniques to reveal such values. However, it will be argued that economic valuation of the environment rests on a misunderstanding of the nature of human preferences and privileges allocational or economic efficiency over other principles. CBA is insensitive to the characteristics of value pluralism and the variety of environmental values.

At both a theoretical and practical level, liberal democratic institutions have been criticised for failing to attend to the importance of democratic deliberation in valuing and decision-making processes. Chapter 3 surveys the recent literature on deliberative democracy. Although there are some weaknesses in the theoretical project, the significance of democratic deliberation is recognised. Particularly important is the space it provides for deliberations and judgements that reflect the plurality of values, including environmental values, in decision-making processes. The arguments of green proponents and critics of deliberative democracy are assessed, and it is argued that greens have good reasons for seeking the institutionalisation of democratic deliberation in the decision-making process.

Much work on deliberative democracy can be criticised on the grounds that it is purely theoretical and speculative, whereas techniques such as CBA, however problematic, are at least a *practical* attempt to internalise environmental values within decision-making processes. It is accepted that the lack of attention to institutional design is a major failing of the deliberative democracy literature. Therefore, the task of Chapter 4 is to assess three potential deliberative models that offer mechanisms by which competing values can be judged. These are: mediation and stakeholder institutions; citizen forums such as deliberative opinion polling, citizens' juries and consensus conferences; and referendums and citizen initiatives. These different models offer interesting insights into how democratic deliberation and reflection on the plurality of environmental values might be enhanced in the policy-making process.

Whereas the primary concern of Chapter 4 is mechanisms to supplement existing decision-making processes, the final chapter develops the analysis of deliberative institutions further. Particular attention is paid to recent work on constitutional environmentalism, representative assemblies and civil society. The thoughts and ideas raised in this final chapter are often speculative, but the central argument is that more imaginative and practical thinking is required from within green political theory on the subject of institutional design that is sensitive to the plurality of environmental values.

1 Value pluralism and the environment

How are we to understand and respond to the clash of values that we experience when trying to make decisions that affect the environment? Should certain environmental values take precedence over other sorts of values in our decisions and judgements? Is there a single environmental ethic that can guide our interventions in the non-human world? We might hope to find answers to these kinds of questions within environmental ethics – the branch of moral philosophy that concerns itself with the relationship between human and non-human entities. Much of the writing within environmental ethics can be seen as a response to the perceived lack of analysis of, and lack of sensitivity towards, the non-human world in traditional ethical and political theorising. However, there are two influential tendencies within environmental ethics that take the debate about the significance of environmental values in a dubious and unhelpful direction. The first of these tendencies is to believe that nature has intrinsic value – a value independent of the contingencies of human valuation. The second tendency is to believe in ethical monism: a desire to generate a single comprehensive environmental ethic that will guide all of our interventions in the non-human world. This chapter explores the problems generated by these two tendencies and offers an alternative conception of how we value the environment. Initially it will suggest that the dichotomy between instrumental and intrinsic value is unnecessarily limiting and that there is a range of environmental values beyond the instrumental use value of the non-human world. Second, ethical monism will be shown to be unsustainable. Value pluralism will be offered as a more effective framework within which to understand this variety of environmental values and better appreciate the value conflicts that arise when deliberating about the environment.

The intrinsic value debate

Environmental ethics emerged in response to environmentally destructive and exploitative attitudes and practices: the 'technocentric ideology' that 'is almost arrogant in its assumption that man is supremely able to understand and control events to suit his purposes' (O'Riordan, 1981: 1). Environmental ethics aims to move away from the human-centred or anthropocentric understanding of the world that has dominated our relations with the environment, and which tends to value nature simply as a resource, as brute matter to be mastered and controlled to fulfil human preferences and desires and increase material affluence. This purely instrumental valuation of nature has been charged with being 'human chauvinist' in its prioritising of human interests over all other considerations and displaying a narrowness of sympathy in failing to take the position of non-human entities into consideration in our ethical reflections and judgements (Midgley, 1994: 111; Routley and Routley, 1995: 105ff.; Hayward, 1998).

According to many green theorists, an alternative orientation towards the non-human world is possible, which recognises and appreciates the interconnectedness of the human and non-human world: ecocentrism (Eckersley, 1992). Here, the human subject is 'decentred' in the sense that a wider range of non-human interests are taken to be significant, and the non-human world – or at least aspects of it – is valued for its own sake rather than simply instrumentally for the achievement of human ends. Perhaps the most influential strategy within ecocentrism, and (arguably) a foundation stone in the development of green political ideology, has been the recognition of *intrinsic* value in non-human nature. The extent to which intrinsic value has influenced green ideas can be witnessed in the work of deep ecologists. Arne Naess, for example, has argued that the principle of 'biospherical egalitarianism' lies at the heart of deep ecology: '*the equal right to live and blossom* is an intuitively clear and obvious value axiom' (Naess, 1973: 95). For Naess, the first principle of the deep ecology movement is that the 'flourishing of human and non-human life on Earth has intrinsic value. The value of non-human life is independent of the usefulness these may have for narrow human purposes' (Naess, 1989: 29). For Naess, life is understood in a broad, non-technical sense, so as to include biologically 'non-living' entities.

The much-quoted 'deep ecology platform' begins with the following three principles:

> The well-being and flourishing of non-human life have intrinsic value, independent of human usefulness.
> The richness and diversity of life contribute to the realisation of these values and are values in themselves.
> Humans have no right to reduce this diversity except to satisfy vital needs.
>
> (Devall and Sessions, 1985: 70)[1]

This brief passage highlights two key aspects of intrinsic value theory. First, the distinction between instrumental and intrinsic value is explicitly drawn. The intrinsic value of nature is independent of any particular value placed on it by humans. Intrinsic value rests on the richness and diversity of the non-human world, and nature has value in and for itself. Second, we can see the powerful implications of such an idea: for deep ecologists the intrinsic value of nature places onerous restrictions on human exploitation and use of the environment. The onus of justification is no longer with those who wish to protect the environment, but rather it is shifted onto those who wish to exploit nature.

This is clearly the strength of the intrinsic value approach: the recognition of such value places a brake on the wanton destruction and exploitation of non-human nature. The isolation of a value that resides in nature challenges the attitude that nature is only valuable in so far as it is directly useful to humanity. The power of intrinsic value for the protection of the environment is obvious.

The idea of intrinsic value may be beguiling and appealing, but sympathetic critics have raised a number of philosophical and practical problems.[2] The belief that nature has intrinsic value generates distinctive problems for understanding the relationship between environmental and other values and, therefore, for making judgements. Given the popularity and influence of intrinsic value theories within green politics, it is important to recognise the limitations of such an approach to our understanding of the value of the environment.

One set of criticisms revolves around isolating the grounds or basis of intrinsic value, deciding which natural entities exhibit intrinsic value and considering whether there are different degrees of intrinsic value. Environmental philosophers offer a range of possible candidates as the characteristic or feature of the natural world that is the basis of moral considerability. Aside from the deep ecological focus on richness and diversity, these have included life (Taylor, 1986; Attfield, 1991), complexity (Mathews, 1991), naturalness (Rolston, 1983; Elliot, 1995) and autopoiesis (Eckersley, 1992).[3] Debates about the grounds of intrinsic value are intimately tied to the question of the type of entity that is to be considered: the aspect of nature that bears the relevant characteristic of moral considerability. Here we discover a series of debates about the entity within which intrinsic value is said to reside: individuals (whether sentient, living or inanimate), species, ecosystems, the biosphere as a whole or some combination of different entities. Precisely what is the bearer of intrinsic value? Which entities exhibit intrinsic value? This ontological question has led to major tensions within environmental philosophy between those who argue that individual animals have intrinsic value, and thus rights (Regan, 1988), and those who argue for a holistic environmental ethic, with intrinsic value resting in species and ecosystems (Callicott, 1995). The problem we are faced with, then, is that there is a plurality of candidates for the grounds of intrinsic value and hence for the natural entities that exhibit such value. If we are required to make judgements about potential interventions in the natural world, it is unclear what aspects of the environment are to be accorded intrinsic value and for what reasons.

The problem of judgement is compounded when we begin to think about how to judge the significance of intrinsic value. Should all entities that exhibit intrinsic value carry the same weight in our judgements or is there a scale of intrinsic value? Can an entity have more, or less, intrinsic value than another entity? Many theorists wish to make the case for a scale of intrinsic value. For example, Robin Attfield relates moral standing to the capacity of entities to live and flourish and then constructs a hierarchy of values based on attributes and capabilities such as sentience, consciousness and cognition (Attfield, 1991). Thus the significance of intrinsic value varies between types of life-forms. Similarly, Freya Mathews relates the degree of intrinsic value to the complexity of living systems (Mathews, 1991: 123).

But, even if we are able to decide on (first) the grounds for intrinsic value, (second) the entities that exhibit intrinsic value and (third) the degree of intrinsic value exhibited by entities, there is a further and perhaps more damaging problem facing intrinsic value theories: our ability to judge the significance of intrinsic value in relation to other values. Is it a value that somehow 'trumps' other types of value that humans may hold? We are being asked to take into account the independent value of the good of a non-human entity. But the very nature of its independence – independent of the contingencies of human valuation – means that we will have problems even recognising this value.

Here we come up against epistemic limits in knowing the good or interests of non-human entities. To what extent can we realistically have access to knowledge of what 'flourishing' might entail for different elements of non-human nature – to know its interests or good beyond the basic conditions of biological functioning? It can be difficult to imaginatively project ourselves into the place of another human being, recognising their interests, needs and capacities. It is an even more formidable exercise to attempt to access and understand the interests and good of non-human entities (Nagel, 1979a). We may have a limited ability to understand the interests of certain domesticated and non-domesticated animals that either share our lives or share similar social natures, but when we move to other living creatures, plants, inanimate objects, species and ecosystems our understanding diminishes rapidly. As Tim Hayward argues: 'There is evident risk that anthropocentrism is merely supplanted by a practice of anthropomorphism – that is imaginatively projecting human characteristics, needs and interests on to other beings which may in fact be radically different from anything humans can imagine' (Hayward, T. 1995: 66). In many cases, we are simply imaginatively projecting our own values and ideals onto non-human entities: after all, the characteristics upon which intrinsic value theories are based are typically those commended within human culture. As Kate Soper contends: 'there is a pervasive inclination to point to humanly admired qualities – its diversity, richness, autonomy and beauty, for example – as those that endow it with 'intrinsic' value' (Soper, 1995: 225).

This hints at a broader problem inherent within intrinsic value theories and the ecocentric stream of thought more generally: anthropocentrism is unavoidable. The very concept of ecocentrism (often cast as 'non-anthropocentrism') may be conceptually and practically contradictory. Within environmental ethics, anthropocentrism is often taken to be the view that only human beings have moral standing, or that it is only the interests of human beings that are significant. This is a crude analysis of the idea and practice of anthropocentrism, focusing attention on one particular (albeit destructive) attitude towards nature. There is a more environmentally enlightened sense of anthropocentrism (often termed 'weak anthropocentrism') in which it is recognised that the interests of, and values associated with, other entities should be taken into account. It is human beings who assign value, but it is not only humans that are of value. The fact that value is assigned or recognised by human beings does not in itself imply that values are anthropocentric in the sense of privileging human beings over the rest of nature. There is nothing inconsistent in human beings valuing the interests of other natural entities above their own. In other words, it is important to distinguish who is asking the questions from who benefits from the answer given (Williams, 1995: 234). Only human beings ask these sorts of questions, and values are to that extent necessarily human based or anthropocentric in the weak sense of the term.

The tendency within environmental ethics to posit intrinsic value in nature thus appears incoherent by failing to appreciate the fundamental role played by human consciousness in recognising and attributing value.[4] As Douglas Torgerson argues, there is a paradoxical quality to ecocentric thought:

> Once we take this ecocentric conception seriously, however, we immediately confront a remarkably ironic paradox. For it is a conception that decenters the human and, at the same time, places humanity at the centre of things. As soon as humanity is expelled from its privileged position, it is readmitted, so to speak, by the back door. Human reason is divested of its pretensions, but placed in judgement of all being.
>
> (Torgerson, 1999: 108)

Environmental philosophers are right to react against the preponderance of an arrogant orientation in which nature is seen simply as something to be mastered and controlled: a strongly anthropocentric or technocentric attitude. However, the appeal to non-anthropocentrism and a focus on intrinsic value in nature is misguided. Recognising humans as valuers does not necessarily imply that only narrowly human-centred values are considerable and significant. Humans may well judge that environmental values take precedence over other human values. The target of ecocentrism needs to be more carefully understood: some form of anthropocentrism is inevitable. What is not inevitable is giving 'exclusive or arbitrary preferential consideration to human interests as opposed to the interests of other beings' (Hayward, 1998: 45). There is, therefore, a significant distance between considering non-human nature only in terms of its instrumental use value for humans (strong anthropocentrism) and the recognition of intrinsic value (ecocentrism). The dangers for greens in focusing so much attention on the intrinsic value of nature are that, first, it is philosophically and practically ambiguous; and, second, it tends to silence other environmental considerations, commitments and values (Taylor, 1996). We can readily understand the attraction of intrinsic value theories in their attempt to place a moral brake on current levels of environmental despoliation and to reorientate our relationship with non-human nature. However, ecocentrism rests on a universal critique of anthropocentrism, thereby criticising human practices and relationships with nature *in toto*. The target needs to be much more specific, focusing on the particular attitudes and practices that tend towards an exploitative attitude towards nature, while recognising that there is a broad range of non-instrumental values that we associate with the non-human world. It is to the variety of environmental values that we now turn.

Reassessing environmental values

Given our criticisms of the tendency within environmental ethics to develop theories based on the recognition of intrinsic value in nature, it is necessary to offer an alternative account of the values associated with the non-human world from within a weak or environmentally enlightened anthropocentric framework. In light of ecocentric critiques, a useful place to begin is with a recognition (and rehabilitation?) of the significance of the instrumental use value of non-human nature.

There is an obvious sense in which the instrumental use of nature is implicit in human life itself. Non-human nature has a direct use value in that it provides the (raw) material conditions for human existence. We draw upon the biological wealth of nature for food, medicines and other goods, but also, more broadly, the life-support function of nature is a precondition for any human activity. Human flourishing is dependent upon the productive, protective and waste-assimilative functions of ecosystems (Dryzek, 1987: 34; Wilson, 1992). Much of the commitment to sustainable development and environmental protection draws its force from this explicit instrumental value. Whether we are talking about existing or future generations, stable environmental conditions and access to adequate environmental resources for the achievement of basic human needs is fundamental. Current and future generations are reliant on the stability of environmental conditions. Again, the potential scientific and medical value of species can provide a strong instrumental case for the preservation of environmental entities that are not obviously useful at present. As Bryan Norton recognises, instrumental valuation of nature creates a persuasive case for the wider preservation of species and ecosystems. The diversity of species is valuable not only for the direct and potential use value of particular species, but also for its contributory value. First, diverse ecosystems provide opportunities for new and potentially useful species to emerge. Second, given our limited and vague knowledge of how complex ecosystems work, the loss of apparently 'useless' species is a potential step towards the collapse of important ecosystems and the loss of 'more useful' entities. There is a danger in undervaluing the contributory value of species and ecosystems to human well-being (Norton, 1986). Although these kinds of arguments do not take us beyond the recognition and valuation of the environment as resource (the instrumental value of the natural world), they do highlight the centrality of the non-human world to our lives and practices. Further, the recognition of how little we understand of the variety and intricacy of ecosystems and the biosphere provides fertile ground for an attitude of humility and prudence towards non-human entities and processes (Norton, 1987: 205; Wilson, 1992: 335).

There is certainly no shame in recognising this use value of the environment, and it can provide a strong rationale for environmental protection. However, according to many intrinsic value theorists, in contemporary societies we typically consider *only* the direct use value of nature. But this is a highly inaccurate picture of the broader values that are associated with the non-human world and does a disservice to human sensibilities and perceptions of nature. The dichotomy between instrumental use value and intrinsic value is unhelpful and leads to a false dilemma, unnecessarily limiting consideration of the full range of interactions between humanity and nature. This can only lead to misrepresentation and an impoverished understanding of human experience and well-being.

If we briefly return to the work of ecocentric theorists, we find that there is a range of characteristics and qualities of the non-human world upon which they have attempted to construct theories of intrinsic value. Part of the criticism of such theories is that they rest on humanly admired characteristics such as diversity, complexity and naturalness. Although misguided in their theoretical ambition, intrinsic value theorists have done us a service in reminding us of significant features of the non-human world: these features are important elements of already existing practices and relationships with the non-human world. There are a range of environmental values that are associated with, for example, aesthetic, scientific, spiritual and cultural practices that enrich our lives.

There is some conceptual difficulty in categorising the types of values that we are interested in here. We are referring not to direct use or exploitation value of the environment, but rather to the non-instrumental values we associate with, for example, a contemplative or reflective orientation towards nature: 'the value which an object has through its ability to contribute to human life by its presence . . . which attaches to things whether alive or not which are interesting to contemplate or heal us when we are with them' (Attfield, 1991: 151–2). Norton, for example, refers to the idea of transformative values, in which aspects of the non-human world provide an occasion for examining or altering preferences as opposed to simply satisfying felt preferences and desires (Norton, 1987: 10). The transformative power of our experiences of nature may 'open our eyes' to new values and 'shape our wants, needs, feelings, emotions, attitudes, sentiments and the like' (McCarthy, 1993: 187). Even under the most extreme conditions, writers and poets have found hope through the contemplation of the beauty of nature. For example, while being held as a political prisoner in intolerable conditions, the poet Irina Ratushinskaya writes in 'I will live and survive':

> And I'll be asked: what helped us to live . . .
> And I will tell of the first beauty
> I saw in captivity.
> A frost covered window! No spyholes, nor walls

Nor cell-bars, nor the long-endured pain -
Only a blue radiance on a tiny pane of glass,
A cast pattern – none more beautiful could be dreamt!
(Ratushinskaya, 1986: 132)

The transformative power of nature is not simple to comprehend, neither is it generalisable: thus its impact on people's preferences and values is not always predictable (Brennan, 1992: 20). We are concerned here with the manner in which the non-human world is constitutive of our well-being rather than simply being a necessary condition for our health and survival. The intention is not to provide a systematic analysis of different environmental values, but simply to draw attention to types of value that are often overlooked because of the oversimplistic intrinsic–instrumental dichotomy.

Take, for example, the manner in which the continuity of natural processes and systems, in particular landscape, plays a part in the development and sustenance of our sense of place. Our lives and practices are ecologically embedded: aspects of non-human nature play a significant role in the constitution of our personal and collective identity and continuing narrative history (Benton, 1993: 180). Ted Benton argues that it is this value of nature that helps to explain 'the disorientation and loss of identity so characteristic of indigenous peoples in the face of ecological destruction and consequent cultural dislocation' (ibid.: 181). A number of indigenous communities, whether in the rainforests of Brazil or Borneo, the prairies of the North Americas or the outback of Australia, have faced such dislocation and environmental loss. Many campaigns against environmental destruction, for example the building of a stretch of motorway through the emblematic Twyford Down in the UK in the early 1990s, can be seen as a direct response to the role that non-human nature can play in the construction of identity. Although this sense of belonging often relates to the environment directly around us, proximity or closeness is not necessarily a spatial issue (Heidegger, 1962: 134ff.): the existence of spatially distant environments may well be constitutive of well-being. It is a sad irony (and perhaps a tragic element of our psychological connections with non-human nature) that often we do not recognise those things that we most value with respect to our own identity until they are irreversibly altered or destroyed: 'the value of particular places or environmental processes may come to be appreciated only when it is seriously threatened' (Grove-White and O'Donovan, 1996: 123).

A number of writers (academic and literary) relate a range of aesthetic, scientific and spiritual values to the capacity of non-human nature to generate a sense of awe and wonder.[5] Contemplation of nature can provide a sense of perspective on our lives and an opportunity to examine and reflect on our preferences and values. R. W. Hepburn, for example, highlights the variety of different properties and aspects of the natural world that can elicit a sense of wonder (Hepburn, 1984: 137–42).[6] The natural world exhibits an obvious range of breathtaking and arresting phenomena, from the grandeur of large-scale spectacular sights, such as sweeping mountain ranges, areas of wilderness and powerful waterfalls, to the intricacy of small-scale, more fragile entities, such as spiders' webs and the patterns of lichens on stone. Beyond these more obvious phenomena, the unintended designs that emerge in nature can be a source of wonder: 'the astonishing variety of living things, the intricacy of their structures and complexity of their behaviour' (Benson, 2000: 72). This relates directly to the sense of wonder that the world is in fact intelligible and explicable, that the natural world can be explained in terms of basic laws of nature. Wonder is certainly an appropriate emotion when considering 'the enormous numbers of conditions, successive and simultaneous, for the emergence of sentient and rational beings' able to appreciate the natural world (Hepburn, 1984: 141). For a number of writers, such as Janna Thompson (1983) and John O'Neill (1993), contact with, and contemplation of, nature can be related directly to the development of creative, aesthetic, scientific and spiritual faculties, generating a strong argument for the preservation of species, habitats and ecosystems.

The recognition of this broad range of environmental values provides critical space for the examination of the attitudes and intentions of those who wantonly destroy or mistreat the natural world, without resorting to the idea of intrinsic value. It is not anthropocentrism per se that is responsible for environmental destruction, but, rather, strong anthropocentric attitudes that misrepresent and distort the value of nature. The critical focus on anthropocentrism or a 'universal humanity' fails to highlight that it is often particularly powerful economic and political interests that are responsible for much environmental destruction. For example, in an analysis of the impact of agriculture on the environment, Soper focuses on the relative power and control over the environment exercised by different social groups: 'the nature in question here ought not to be spoken of as if it were the product of some universal "human" subject, since it has acquired the form it has in virtue of divisive and inegalitarian social and sexual relations of production, in other words, in virtue of historically specific cultural forces' (Soper, 1995: 137).[7] A purely exploitative orientation towards nature reflects an inhumane disposition and a failure to develop specifically human capacities of perception. For many theorists, the recognition of a wide range of environmental values can be directly related to particular characteristics and virtues necessary for the protection of the environment. Hepburn, for example, contends that the life-enhancing, non-exploitative and non-utilitarian character of wonder has a close affinity to ethical attitudes 'that seek to affirm and respect other-being'. He relates wonder to virtues such as compassion, gentleness and humility, the absence of which typically signal an indifference towards nature (Hepburn, 1984: 145–6).[8] As John Barry contends: 'The importance of virtues for the green position resides in the necessity of self-restraint, prudence and foresight so that long term (i.e. sustainable) well-being is not sacrificed or undermined by desires to satisfy immediate self-interest' (Barry, 1999: 35).

Ethical monism

The second tendency within environmental ethics that is challenged in this chapter is the commitment to ethical monism, the belief that there is a single, comprehensive and systematic theory that will eliminate indeterminacy and value conflict. Judgement proceeds by evaluating competing values against overarching criteria. Within environmental ethics, ethical monism can take two forms: either there is a single ethic to guide our interventions in the non-human worlds; or, even more challenging, a single ethical theory can explain all our interactions, both those between humans and between human and non-human worlds. In many cases, it is theorists who support the concept of intrinsic value who offer such monistic theories, although there is no necessary connection between intrinsic value and ethical monism.

Ethical monism is not something unique to environmental ethics: the desire that there should be 'one canonical, homogenous ethical language' is common within mainstream moral philosophy (Williams,

1996: 32). Within both the broader field of moral philosophy and environmental ethics itself, the defence and refutation of competing systematic theories is one of the principal preoccupations, carried out in the belief that we will eventually discover irrefutable arguments in favour of one particular theoretical approach, whether Kantian, utilitarian, neo-Aristotelian or whatever. Exemplification becomes a constant feature of debates within moral philosophy, in which hypothetical situations, more and more obscure and fantastic examples, are created that expose the weaknesses and contradictions of opposing ethical theories. Much time is spent by proponents refining theories to account for particularly obscure possibilities and to create an ethical theory which can deal with all potential situations. Within environmental ethics, perhaps the best known and most discussed of these thought experiments is Richard and Val Routley's 'last man' example: is it right for the last man surviving the collapse of the world system to lay waste to the environment around him, eliminating every living entity (Benson, 2000: 18–28)?[9]

Examples of monistic approaches within environmental ethics abound. For example, both Attfield (1991) and Paul Taylor (1986) offer monistic theories to guide our ethical judgements, based on the intrinsic value of all living organisms (animals and plants). However, the different theories can lead to differing judgements, given that Attfield's is a consequentialist theory that holds that there are differing degrees of intrinsic value in different kinds of life forms, whereas Taylor's neo-Kantian theory argues for equal respect for all living organisms. Writers such as J. Baird Callicott (1995) and Laura Westra (1989) attempt to move beyond attention to life forms, offering monistic theories that combine a holistic respect for ecological systems and processes with respect for individual organisms. Callicott exemplifies the tendency towards ethical monism in environmental ethics when he states that environmental philosophers are:

> looking for a moral theory that would enfranchise natural entities as a whole ... an ethic ... which situates the environment as the object, not merely the arena, of human moral concern ... By working with *one* ethical theory, chosen to accommodate our special concern for the environment, how could we also account for our traditional interpersonal responsibilities and social duties, accommodate all these intermediate new moral concerns to boot,

and then order, and mutually reconcile the whole spectrum of traditional and novel ethical domains?

(Callicott, 1990: 99–100)

As with the desire to locate intrinsic value theory, discussed earlier, the rationale behind such a theoretical adventure is easily understood: in this case the overcoming of conflict and indeterminacy. However, contrary to the assumptions of monistic approaches, why should we assume that there will be such a coherent, canonical account of value? Why should we expect to have a clear decision rule or principle that negotiates us through tensions between the values we associate with, for instance, individual non-human entities, species or ecosystems? There is a plurality of different types of environmental entity and a plurality of values that we associate with the non-human world – use, life-support, aesthetic, cultural, spiritual, etc. At times, these values are likely to conflict with each other and with non-environmental values. Should we expect a definitive answer on how to balance the claims of social justice, intergenerational equity and environmental protection implicit within sustainable development? Will the same ethical theory provide a definitive judgement on whether the preservation of a landscape should take precedence over the economic development that could lead from the building of a new road scheme? Can this single theory judge the merits of the development of wind turbines against the possible impact on particular bird species and habitats? Can it realistically accommodate the different values we associate with individual organisms of varying complexity, inanimate objects, species, ecosystems and the biosphere as a whole? As Mary Midgley has argued: 'We have to arbitrate all sorts of local inter-species conflicts; we do not have a tidy system of Rights and Duties that will always tell us how to do so. But then, did anybody ever suppose that we did have one, even on the human scene?' (Midgley, 1994: 112).

Given the diverse and complex nature of our moral inheritance, it is far from clear why we should expect ethical judgements to be conceptually simple, based on a unitary account of value that will overcome dilemmas and conflicts (Williams, 1985; Taylor, 1989). A diversity of moral sources and traditions have affected our thinking about the environment and given rise to the diversity of different positions within the environmental movement, from deep ecologists to nature conservationists (Passmore, 1980; Soper, 1995; Connelly and Smith, 2003). To 'overcome' this diversity and complexity would be to lose much of the richness of human–non-human interactions and impose a false unity on the plurality of values and goods we associate with the environment. Instead of searching for an all-inclusive monistic theory, a more realistic framework within which to understand the plurality of environmental (and non-environmental) values might be value pluralism.[10]

Value pluralism

Value pluralism rests on two ideas: the *incompatibility* of values and the *incommensurability* of values. The incompatibility of values refers to situations in which two (or more) possible actions, ideals or virtues cannot be fulfilled at the same time; the incommensurability of values recognises that there may be no common value, principle or decision rule against which conflicting values can be weighed or evaluated. We will investigate these two ideas in turn.

According to Thomas Nagel, conflict can and does occur between different types of values, for instance between and among competing obligations, rights, utility, perfectionist ends and private commitments (Nagel, 1979b: 128; also Williams, 1981: 72–6). Such conflicts may be within a single person or between persons. Value pluralism recognises the incompatibility of many values and goods and the sense of loss or 'moral remainder' that can occur when having to chose one course of action over other possibilities (Williams, 1973a: 166–86). Incompatibility is fundamental to the human condition: we simply cannot fulfil all desirable actions, ideals and virtues.

Incompatibility is common in the types of conflict familiar within environmental politics. The actions and values of advocates of ever-increasing levels of economic growth and of environmentalists are, at times, going to conflict. For example, a proposal to build a road through an ecologically sensitive habitat leads to a conflict of values that is incompatible: a conflict between protection of the environment and increased mobility and economic development opportunities. And it is not simply a matter of environmentalists versus the rest! Value conflicts emerge between environmentalists. Take, for example, the highly controversial siting of wind turbines. Frequently, the best location for such renewable energy providers is on much cherished exposed hillsides or coastal bird habitats, leading to conflict between groups all coveting the environmentalist mantle. Again, the different ideals embodied within the concept of sustainable development frequently pull in different directions. Trying to balance the demands of justice to present, and future, generations with environmental protection leads to compromise between often incompatible values. What would maximise the fulfilment of one of these values is likely to be at the expense of the other two. Different conceptions of sustainable development – whether ecological modernisation, Third World development or bioregionalism – will balance and prioritise the values we associate with social justice, intergenerational equity and non-human nature in different ways, thus leading to conflicting and incompatible ideas about the direction of environmental policy. As Soper argues: 'green politics needs to recognise that it is appealing not to a single, but to a plurality of values, the mutual compatibility of which is by no means obvious and certainly needs to be displayed rather than merely assumed' (Soper, 1995: 251).

Value incompatibility explains why greens offer a variety of conflicting accounts of the good life and why potentially conflicting elements of different visions can be appealing. Any way of life entails prioritising certain values over others and choosing certain courses of action at the expense of other possibilities (Hampshire, 1983). The ecological and social requirements of sustainability do not determine a single way of life; rather they leave open a wide range of potentially sustainable alternatives (Benton, 1993: 180–1; Barry, 1999: 259). Value conflict and incompatibility is endemic within environmental politics.

The second element of value pluralism is the incommensurability of values: 'in its most general formulation, incommensurability refers to a disruption in communication across theories, vocabularies, or perspectives that renders rational assessment difficult or impossible' (Furrow, 1995: 28–9). When, in reasoning about the qualities (ethical and non-ethical) of a particular situation, we find ourselves drawn in different and conflicting directions, there may be no common value, principle or decision rule against which the opposing values can be weighed and evaluated. This point is forcefully made by Bernard Williams: 'It is not true that for each conflict of values, there is some value which can be appealed to (independent or not) in order rationally to resolve the conflict' (Williams, 1981: 77). However, this does not force us to accept the stronger thesis of radical incomparability that 'no conflict of values can ever rationally be resolved' (ibid.; also Raz, 1986: 329). Acceptance of incommensurability leads us to realise that, in cases of value conflict, conflicting values cannot necessarily be reduced to one another, to some common feature or to an independent standard.[11]

In the Introduction, we discussed the different ways that the rainforest is valued: the idea of incommensurability, it now appears, helps us to understand why our judgements about such an environment are often pulled in different and conflicting directions. John O'Neill's discussion of the value of a wetland provides a similar example of value conflict (O'Neill, 1993: 107–9; 1997: 75–7). We can make a series of different judgements about the value of such a location. For example, in judging its value as a landscape, we will evoke aesthetic criteria and look to the judgement of poets and artists. To judge its scientific value, we would appeal to scientific practices and accord the ecologist authority. Judging its economic, spiritual or cultural value will require an appeal to different sets of criteria and practices. Importantly though, aesthetic, scientific and other types of judgement are incommensurable:

> The values appealed to for the appraisal of the site under the description of habitat, such as species richness and integrity, are distinct from those appealed to for its appraisal as a landscape or place. None seems reducible to others, nor to some other common value. None straightforwardly takes precedence over others: there is no privileged canonical description for the purposes of an over-arching evaluation. The different appraisals of the site call upon an irreducible pluralism of values.
>
> (O'Neill, 1997: 77)

Thus, any environmental good is likely to pull us in different directions when we discuss its value: they might be termed 'mixed value entities' (Raz and Griffin, 1991, 86ff.; Brennan, 1992: 28). And this causes conflict when trying to compare the value of different non-human entities. For example, how are we to evaluate the relative worth of two different locations if one is a species-rich habitat and the other an awe-inspiring landscape? An evaluation of relative worth would depend upon which criterion is used – beauty or diversity (O'Neill, 1993: 108–9). Given the incommensurability of value, and thus a level of indeterminacy, we are left with the burden of judgement.

It becomes clear why the quest for an overarching, monistic environmental ethic that enfranchises nature is so seductive. A strategy that is able to isolate and prioritise a particular environmental value, that provides an unambiguous vision of the green good life and/or that provides a framework within which to adjudicate between different values will avoid indeterminacy and moral dilemmas. This is certainly at the heart of Callicott's vision of 'a moral theory that would enfranchise natural entities as a whole . . . and mutually reconcile the whole spectrum of traditional and novel ethical domains' (Callicott, 1990: 99–100).

Value pluralism offers itself as an alternative to this 'drive toward a *rationalistic conception of rationality*' (Williams, 1985: 18). Although ethical monism is incredibly seductive in its simplicity, such a 'quest for commensuration' (Rorty, 1980: 317) misrepresents the diversity of our experiences and values. It is in this sense that Williams views the enterprise of 'constructing a philosophical *ethical theory* (in the sense of systematising moral belief)' as a misguided one. An unwarranted model of theoretical rationality and adequacy is introduced into the realm of moral belief in an attempt to remove uncertainty and reduce conflicts (Williams, 1981: 80).

Value conflicts and dilemmas are not pathological, but are an integral feature of the ethical life of individuals and groups. The incompatibility and incommensurability of values and the conflict this can engender does not represent a failure of reasoning and judgement. However, the existence of these characteristics does have important consequences and implications for how we understand the nature of judgement.

Judgement in the face of value pluralism

When making judgements, different values often pull us in different directions, and there is no standard or common currency against which competing values can be assessed. Value pluralism recognises the indeterminacy of reason endemic in ethical judgements. This does not entail indifference, rather that conflicting judgements prioritise different values and are supported by different kinds of reasons and justifications.[12] The failure of reason to produce a single objectively right answer means that a judgement may often be accompanied by sense of loss, regret, discomfort or hesitation, the intensity of which will be dependent on the significance of the judgement in hand.[13] Conflicts can vary from the tragic to the trivial, and the sense of loss need not be a pathological feature of ethical judgement terms, but may be a result of the recognition that choice may disable the pursuit of other possibilities and values: 'life is impoverished in certain respects, but enriched in others' (Raz, 1986: 353).

A further complicating factor for our understanding of judgement is that when we judge we do so from a particular perspective or horizon, defined by our commitments and identifications (Taylor, 1989: 27; Hampshire, 1989: 119; D'Agostino, 1990: 452; Owen, 1995: 38–9). O'Neill's wetland example highlights how judgements are affected by the perspective of the valuer, in this case whether we are interested in landscape or ecology. Again, the value of the rainforest, discussed in the Introduction, will vary from a conservationist or preservationist perspective. The weighting that different agents give to the differing values associated with environmental entities will be dependent upon the particular perspective and form of life from which they judge. A field ecologist, a cultural historian, a landscape artist and a local inhabitant may well come to quite different evaluations as to which of the values associated with the wetland or rainforest are most significant. Such judgements can be well reasoned and publicly accessible but at the same time conflict with one another.

This is not, however, to claim that judgements are radically subjective; that there are no standards of judgement; that we are faced with indifferent relativism. To comprehend another's judgement is to attempt to understand the perspective from which they judge, and, through such an attempt, one's own perspective becomes a matter for reflection. Through understanding the judgement of others we come to recognise that our own perspectives may be limited and fallible, in that certain values may be ignored or misrepresented. The more we appreciate and take into account the perspectives of others, the richer our judgements will be.[14]

It is only through encountering other perspectives and value orientations that we are able to come to reflective judgements. No single individual will privately express the diversity of environmental values. The development of what Hannah Arendt terms an 'enlarged mentality' (Arendt, 1982: 42–3) appears essential if we are to come to consider and understand the way that others value different aspects of the environment and other goods:

> such judgement must liberate us from the 'subjective private conditions', that is, from the idiosyncrasies which determine the outlook of each individual in his privacy and are legitimate as long as they are only privately held opinions, but are not fit to enter the market place, and lack all validity in the public realm. And this enlarged way of thinking, which as judgement knows how to transcend its own individual limitations . . . cannot function in strict isolation or solitude; it needs the presence of others in whose place it must think, whose perspectives it must take into consideration, and without whom it never has the opportunity to operate at all.
>
> (Arendt, 1968: 220–1)

The development of enlarged mentality requires the exercise of imagination: a necessary condition for putting ourselves in the position of others and distancing ourselves from private conditions and circumstances that limit and inhibit the exercise of judgement (Arendt, 1982: 68).[15] Faced with the plurality of values we associate with the environment and the plurality of perspectives from which situations are judged, the development of an enlarged mentality is fundamental. The exercise of judgement does not mean that conflict will be overcome; rather that judgements will not be based solely on individual resources and private considerations, but will benefit from the knowledge, experience and insights of others (Waldron, 1999: 93).

We are faced with living alongside people with different perspectives on the significance of environmental values. But, we need common action on enterprises such as protecting the environment. It is this need for common action, and the potential for disagreement as to what any common decision should be, that Jeremy Waldron terms the 'circumstances of politics' (Waldron, 1999: 154–5). The question that faces us, then, is how to structure our political institutions in the face of such plurality.

Conclusion

For many environmental ethicists, the acceptance of indeterminacy, conflict and contradiction in judgements is an acceptance of failure: there may appear to be a plurality of environmental values, but the conflict this can engender can nonetheless be overcome though the identification of intrinsic value in nature and/or the 'serious business of searching for the Holy Grail of environmental ethics – the coherent, inclusive super-theory' (Callicott, 1990: 105). This chapter has been highly sceptical about the ideas of intrinsic value and ethical monism: both tend to limit the consideration of the variety of relationships between humanity and non-human nature. These two tendencies will likely misrepresent and distort the plurality of values and goods associated with the human condition: we will have an impoverished sense of the variety of relations that exist between humans and non-human entities. And, in the process, environmental ethics evades the fundamental task of offering insights into how we are to mediate between the plethora of environmental and non-environmental values (Taylor, 1996: 95).

In recognising the characteristics of incompatibility and incommensurability, value pluralism helps us to comprehend the divisions we experience within the environmental movement and at sites of environmental conflict. But it does not do what many within environmental ethics hope – it does not provide a comprehensive and systematic framework within which we can definitively assess the 'rightness' or 'goodness' of human interventions in the environment. The situation is confused and conflictual. There is a diversity of values (environmental and non-environmental) that we appeal to in making judgements. Value pluralism does not banish disagreement and conflict through the creation of a sophisticated theoretical framework. In order that policy decisions that affect the environment reflect the plurality of relevant values, it is thus imperative that we turn our attention towards the question of institutional design. Specifically, how are we to create the conditions which promote the development of an enlarged mentality? How do we structure political institutions and decision-making processes that are sensitive to the plurality of values we associate with the non-human world and which can accommodate the challenge of value incompatibility and incommensurability? Given that value pluralism points to there not being a single green ethical position per se, what institutional form might allow for divergent and conflicting values to be articulated and considered? Discussion of this is the task of the rest of the book.

2 Environmental economics and the internalisation of environmental values

How do liberal democratic institutions respond to the plurality of environmental values? How do they ensure that policy decisions effectively reflect the array of values held by citizens? One of the most favoured appraisal techniques within contemporary political institutions is cost–benefit analysis (CBA), which provides a comparison of economic costs and benefits of proposed policies, programmes and projects. CBA appears to have a number of advantages as a decision rule; in particular it realises two principles that are highly valued within contemporary polities. First, it embodies the liberal democratic desire that decisions should be based on the aggregation of individuals' preferences (Miller, 1992: 54; Phillips, 1995: 149). As David Pearce argues: 'That human preferences should count and be "sovereign" is the fundamental value judgement of CBA' (Pearce, 1998: 87). Second, the method of aggregation of preferences within CBA generates results that embody the principle of allocational or economic efficiency. 'Value for money' is the guiding decision rule.

The use of CBA is becoming increasingly entrenched in the decision-making processes of democratic governments, and in environmental policy in particular. Since the Reagan administration in the United States instituted the requirement of a CBA for all major regulations in 1981, legislation and executive orders have expanded the Environmental Protection Agency's (EPA) obligation to articulate the costs and benefits of environmental policies and regulations (National Center for Environmental Economics, 2001).[1] In the UK, the Environment Agency was mandated under the Environment Act (1996) to undertake a CBA for all policy proposals (Pearce, 1998). In order to ensure that such assessments include the full range of costs and benefits, there is growing pressure to expand the coverage of CBA to consistently include monetarised costs and benefits of environmental impacts. Environmental economists have developed ever more sophisticated techniques so that the monetary value of environmental effects can be internalised within calculations.[2]

This chapter investigates the nature of the techniques used by environmental economists to evaluate environmental impacts, and challenges their internalisation within CBA calculations. It is argued that such economic valuation is based on a misunderstanding of the nature of human preferences and privileges allocational or economic efficiency over other principles. The theoretical and pragmatic defence of the economic valuation of the environment is insensitive to the plurality of values that we associate with the non-human world. Decisions that draw heavily on the use of extended CBA will misrepresent our environmental values and commitments.

Economic valuation of the environment

In the UK (and elsewhere), the work of Pearce and his colleagues has been particularly influential in promoting the internalisation of environmental externalities within CBA, especially since the publication of *Blueprint for a Green Economy* (1989), originally a report commissioned by the Minister for the Environment, Chris Patten.[3] This directly influenced the development of the then Department of the Environment's *Policy Appraisal and the Environment* (1991), which contained detailed guidance promoting the monetary valuation of environmental effects of policy and programme options within decision-making procedures across Whitehall.[4] The document states:

> In cost–benefit analysis as many impacts as possible are expressed in terms of the monetary value that society places on them, and the net benefit is derived as the basis for policy choices . . . . One significant advantage is that most policy analyses use monetary or financial values for many effects, and the valuation of environmental impacts puts them on a similar footing.
>
> (Department of the Environment, 1991: 23)

An indication of the growing influence of environmental economics is the explicit support of economic valuation of the environment within the Treasury's *Appraisal and Evaluation in Central Government* (otherwise known as 'The Green Book'): 'The identification and, where possible, valuation of environmental costs and benefits, has become still more important with the acceptance of a policy of "sustainable development"' (HM Treasury, 1997: 45).[5] However, the extent of the institutionalisation of extended-CBA in the policy assessment process across Whitehall remains inconsistent, although a more systematic use is starting to happen (for examples, see Pearce, 1998: 92–3). According to environmental economists, many ecologically-insensitive policies and projects may well not have gone ahead if environmental externalities had been incorporated within economic analysis.[6] For instance, Jean-Phillipe Barde and David Pearce offer the infamous case of the motorway (M3) extension through Twyford Down, the much celebrated first site of systematic direct action against road building in the UK in the 1990s. They argue that, if the CBA for the road proposal had included the economic valuation of the aesthetic worth of the area, then the cutting would have been unlikely to proceed on economic grounds and other options would have been viewed as more economically efficient (Barde and Pearce, 1991: 1–2).

Although there is a family of techniques and justifications associated with CBA (Nash *et al.*, 1975: 126–31; Copp, 1985: 129ff.), government guidance follows the conventional approach whereby changes in individuals' welfare, represented by their willingness to pay (WTP) for an intervention or willingness to accept (WTA) compensation, are aggregated. For an intervention to be judged favourably, the net present value (NPV) should be positive – the net benefits should outweigh the net costs, the costs and benefits having been 'discounted'. A discount rate is applied to take into account the time at which costs and benefits accrue – it is argued that individuals are impatient and have a time preference for immediate gains in well-being over their postponement to a future occasion (Pearce and Turner, 1990: 211ff.). The preferred policy option is the one with the highest NPV (HM Treasury, 1997: 10).

The decision rule that operates is termed the Kaldor–Hicks compensation test, or potential Pareto optimality. The compensation test derives from the theoretically compelling idea of Pareto optimality, which holds that an outcome is Pareto optimal when it results in an increase in utility across society without any individuals' utility being reduced.[7] The Pareto-optimal outcome is the one that is most economically efficient. Practically, though, particularly at the level of public policy, it is very difficult to imagine that an intervention would not negatively affect someone's welfare (or utility function). Thus, John Hicks and Nicholas Kaldor (independently) developed the principle of *potential* Pareto optimality, whereby 'a policy is to be judged socially beneficial if the gainers secure sufficient by way of benefits such that they can compensate the losers and still have some net gain left over' (Pearce and Nash, 1981: 2). Conventionally then, projects or policies should only be taken forward if they produce a positive NPV, thereby demonstrating potential Pareto improvements. There is a tendency to view the option with the largest NPV as the most economically efficient. There is an intuitive appeal in the principles that underlie CBA: as a decision rule it embodies the liberal desire to take individuals' (pre-given) preferences seriously and to make a collective choice based on the aggregation of these individual preferences.

Environmental economists have proved to be sensitive to different types of environmental value that they take to be elements of individual preferences. Thus, the total economic value of any environmental good can be derived from the addition of the 'actual use', 'option' and 'existence' values (Pearce *et al*, 1989: 60–3; Pearce and Turner, 1990: 129–40). Following Pearce and his colleagues, actual use value is taken to be equivalent to the instrumental value of the environment: the quantification of the benefits derived by those who make direct use of non-human nature. Option value includes a number of distinct elements. First, it takes into account the willingness to pay for the preservation of an entity in the likelihood that the individual may make use of it in the future. Second, it includes the desire to conserve the environment for future generations (often referred to as bequest value). Third, it incorporates the pleasure secured in the knowledge that others derive a value from the entity in question. Existence value is the quantification of 'non-instrumental' environmental values: 'concern for, sympathy with, respect for the rights or welfare of non-human beings and the values of which are unrelated to human use' (Pearce and Turner, 1990: 130).

A range of sophisticated techniques has been developed to generate environmental values and these are typically separated into two types: revealed and stated preference methods.[8] The revealed preference, or surrogate market, approach attempts to derive the monetary value of environmental benefits or costs from individual behaviour in actual markets. For instance, the hedonic pricing method assesses the influence that environmental conditions (such as air quality, landscape or noise) have on house prices, or the premium that employees will accept to work in an environmentally risky workplace; the travel cost method assesses the costs that individuals incur in visiting environmental amenities. These techniques are limited in applicability and incorporate contested assumptions. For example, the hedonic pricing method assumes that the property and labour markets function freely and that individuals are fully informed about, and in an economic position to respond to, environmental conditions. The travel cost method assumes that any travel time is viewed only as a cost and neglects the values of those who either have chosen to live close by or who do not or cannot visit the amenity but still value its existence.

Given the perceived unreliability of revealed preference techniques and the number of situations in which no market information exists on the value of environmental entities, environmental economists have tended to concentrate on stated or expressed preference techniques such as contingent valuation (CV). This technique creates hypothetical market conditions in which valuations are elicited through interview. By making 'bids', individuals express their WTP for environmental improvement or WTA compensation for a loss of environmental quality. CV is receiving a great deal of attention within environmental economics, both because it has potentially wide applicability over many areas of environmental concern and because it enables economists to distinguish between aspects of the total economic value of environmental entities (use, option and existence values).[9] CV has been used to evaluate local landscapes, endangered species and even climate change.

However, environmental economists have identified a wide variety of possible sources for bias within CV.[10] The first of these is strategic bias, the temptation to 'free ride' on the WTP of others. This is a long-standing concern in the economic analysis of public good provision, wherein individuals understate their actual preferences in the belief that they will obtain benefits in excess of the costs that they will have to pay. Second, the design of CV surveys has affected results in at least three ways: starting point bias, which stems from any example bids offered by the interviewer; vehicle bias, which indicates sensitivity to the instrument of payment, such as taxation, entrance fees, surcharges or higher prices; and information bias, which reflects the amount and quality of information provided during the interview. Finally, a hypothetical bias may result from the differing features of hypothetical and actually existing market transactions, and an operational bias from being unfamiliar with valuing the good in question by making economic bids.

Economists have also witnessed two other perplexing types of results in attempts to generate economic valuations of environmental goods. First, a number of studies have 'reported a high frequency of protest, zero or inordinately large dollar-value responses to questions' (Vadnjal and O'Connor, 1994: 369–70). Citizens have not always responded in the way that economists expect. Second, it is not uncommon to find that there is a wide discrepancy between WTA compensation and WTP for environmental improvements, with the former consistently being several times higher (Knetsch, 1994: 352). This differential can have a significant effect on policy decisions since there is a theoretical assumption that WTP and WTA are equivalent and techniques for deriving environmental values tend to be based on WTP – consistently the lower of the two valuations. For example, in the discussion of environmental valuation in 'The Green Book', the UK Treasury advises: 'Non-marketed goods are generally best valued in terms of people's willingness to pay for marginal changes in supply' (HM Treasury, 1997: 46). The privileging of WTP is thus likely to encourage more environmentally destructive policies: 'losses are understated, standards are set at inappropriate levels, policy selections are biased, too many environmentally degrading activities are encouraged, and too few mitigation efforts are undertaken' (Knetsch, 1990: 227).

Typically, environmental economists believe that biases within CV can be eliminated, given more research and greater sensitivity in surveying. However, these biases may in fact be symptomatic of a misunderstanding of the nature and diversity of values that we associate with the non-human world.

Challenging economic valuation and extended cost–benefit analysis

We have already admitted that there is an intuitive appeal in the use of CBA, to the idea that social decisions should be based on the aggregation of costs and benefits to the members of society, including environmental effects. This welfare economic procedure has its roots firmly in a utilitarian heritage, which attempts to respond to a world characterised by moral diversity. Given the lack of a uniting moral framework, utilitarianism offers an impersonal method of arriving at social and political decisions. The diversity of first-order values are judged in terms of a second order value, utility. Individuals' utility functions can then be aggregated and alternative policy options compared.[11] As Raymond Plant argues:

> Utilitarianism provides a second order way of resolving . . . first order moral conflicts. People may have a wide range of wants and preferences which will be influenced by their particular moral outlook. Utilitarianism resolves these conflicts by the neutral and impersonal rule that of all the policies available to government, the one which is likely in its consequences to procure the greatest amount of want satisfaction is the course which should be chosen.
>
> (Plant, 1991: 140–1)

There are, however, a number of theoretical problems with the use of such a utilitarian approach to collective decision making, particularly when it is extended to include environmental valuations. In this section, we shall focus attention on two aspects of the theoretical framework underpinning CBA: the nature of individual preferences and the status of allocational efficiency in collective choice.

The nature of individual preferences

Cost–benefit analysis rests on the assumption that individuals make judgements about states of affairs primarily in terms of their own well-being. Here, we witness the clearest indication of the influence of utilitarian thought in economic theorising: the abstract and idealised conception of a person, *homo economicus*, from which economic modelling progresses.[12] Individuals are taken to be calculating utility maximisers with given and fully ordered preferences (Hollis, 1994: 116). It is assumed that individuals have both full information and are rational such that they will calculate and choose that option which will maximise their individual preferences. Environmental preferences (like other preferences) can be discovered through the analysis of an individual's behaviour in market situations (revealed preferences) or, for situations in which this is not possible, through stated- or expressed-preference techniques.

Individual preferences are shaped by a number of factors that will affect either behaviour in existing markets or responses in CV. First, individual decisions are typically made in conditions of information scarcity and thus cannot hope to approach the economic ideal of rationality. Environmental economists have recognised that the type of information provided affects responses. Second, social and economic constraints impose themselves on individual behaviour and choices. An individual may not be in an economic or social position to act on information (this is one of the limitations of hedonic pricing), or their sense of what is possible may be restricted. As Bernard Williams argues: 'What one wants, or is capable of wanting, is itself the function of numerous social forces, and importantly rests on a sense of what is possible. Many a potential desire fails to become an express preference because the thought is absent that it would ever be possible to achieve' (Williams, 1973b: 147).[13]

It is difficult to imagine how these contextual factors could be overcome through the refinement of valuation techniques alone.[14] However, even if this were possible, the preferences generated by both revealed- and stated-preference techniques are not entirely legitimate because they fail to appreciate the nature of our judgements about the non-human world and assume that different values are commensurable and reducible to an economic value.

Theoretically, the valuations within a CBA ought simply to be based on an individual's judgement concerning the maximisation of his or her own well-being or utility. However, as Russell Keat recognises, environmental valuations are likely to include a number of ethical judgements that undermine this basic assumption of economic analysis. Option value and existence value (see earlier), isolated by environmental economists, relate to concerns over the distribution of environmental goods among both current and future generations, and to the non-instrumental value of environmental entities. Concern for the well-being of others can be understood in broadly utilitarian terms, but its inclusion within individual preferences leads to 'double counting' when preferences are aggregated (Keat, 1997: 39–40). More damaging still is the recognition that, when preferences include judgements relating to non-instrumental environmental values, then the conceptual framework of CBA is being stretched to breaking point. As Amartya Sen argues: 'choice may reflect a compromise among a variety of considerations of which personal welfare may be just one' (Sen, 1977: 324). Ethical and aesthetic judgements are being represented as if they were simply judgements about personal welfare. For Keat, this failure to recognise different types of judgement means that 'the use of the extended form of CBA cannot be justified; for this involves the conceptual/categorial error of treating ethical judgements as if they were judgements about the well-being of those who make them' (Keat, 1997: 39).

This returns us to the idea of incommensurability raised in Chapter 1: environmental and other values are often incommensurable, and the representation of these different values by a single yardstick or measuring rod, in this case a monetary valuation, is illegitimate. It is argued in *Policy Appraisal and the Environment* that 'a monetary standard is a convenient means of expressing the relative values which society places on different uses of resources' (Department of the Environment, 1991: 23). The monetary standard may be 'convenient', but is it possible to translate different kinds of values into monetary terms? Environmental economists readily admit that there is a diversity of values associated with the non-human world, and offer distinctions between actual use, option values and existence values. However, the application of a monetary value to represent these different values generates much dispute. The purpose of seeking these valuations is to represent our ethical commitments to future generations and to the non-instrumental values we associate with the non-human world. But it is a distortion of the nature of such ethical relations to assume that they can be understood using the same criterion as is used for economic valuations. Aesthetic and ethical considerations are qualitatively different from economic valuations. What, after all, does the economic value of an obligation to future generations, or of the commitment to the preservation of aspects of the non-human world, actually mean? That economists generate a monetary value is unquestionable; what precisely that value represents is another matter. Obligations, duties and commitments are judged by other criteria than utility. They refer to different aspects of the human condition and as such are not necessarily commensurable or compatible with one another.[15]

The idea that values are commensurable and can be represented by an economic value is intimately connected to the principle of substitutability that is fundamental to weaker conceptions of sustainability. There is an assumption that 'human', 'human-made' and 'natural' capital can be substituted for one another. For example, the value of a landscape is equivalent to a certain amount of money and, as such, its loss can be adequately compensated. Alternatively, the landscape, a church and a section of road that have the same economic valuation are hence taken to be, in a strong sense, equivalent: if they have the same (total) economic value, they are therefore substitutable. The incommensurability and incompatibility theses offer grounds for strong objections to such an assumption. Obviously, compensation can be paid for the loss of a landscape. But it is just that: compensation. The monetary value is not equivalent to the plurality of values associated with the landscape. Entities as diverse as a stretch of road, a church, a landscape or a particular ecosystem may have equivalent *economic* value, but this in no way means that they have the same *total* value. We can, for example, ascertain the market value of a piece of land, but its broader value clearly goes well beyond that. Economic analysis cannot adequately address the sense of place that a landscape provides for a community, the link it symbolises with past generations, or other aesthetic and perhaps spiritual values. The economists' scale is partial, and distorts the particularity of different types of goods and values which may be both incommensurable and incompatible.[16]

The application of discounting to individual preferences within CBA confuses matters even further. Discounting assumes that all the environmental values elicited by economists relate to the future in the same way. But the values we associate with aesthetic, ethical, cultural or scientific considerations do not have the same temporal form as economic values. Our aesthetic or ethical sensibility is misunderstood if it is seen to rest on a desire for immediate gratification that is implicit within economic reasoning. The idea that ethical commitments to future generations should be discounted perhaps reaches new levels of absurdity. The incommensurability thesis implies that different values and modes of association with the non-human world have different temporal features. There are grounds for challenging not only the assumption that qualitatively different values can be represented by a monetary value but also that they then should be treated as economic commodities when compared over time.

Pearce is obviously exasperated about citizens who refuse to cooperate with the CV process and believe that placing a dollar value on the environment 'debases' nature. He argues that: 'Far from "debasing" the environment, the use of the money metric is there to establish the fact that the correct context is one of trade-off, whether it is expressed in terms of costs and benefits, or competing ethical values' (Pearce, 1998: 97). Pearce is right that judgements often require a trade-off between different values or alternatives. However, the dispute rests on whether trade-offs are best represented in monetary terms. Such a representation of competing values misrepresents the very nature of environmental (and other) values and leads to a distorted judgement of relative worth. There is evidence that the refusal of some respondents to cooperate with the CV process and the lodging of zero or inordinately large bids indicates that individuals are often unable and/or unwilling to judge environmental values in a manner which reduces judgement to a question of utility maximisation and assumes that values are commensurable. These may not be 'errors' to be ignored, as economists might wish, but may be instead a recognition on the part of respondents that the valuation process is attempting to shape their judgements in unacceptable ways. An ecologically sensitive disposition is poorly represented by a measurement of individual utility. Respondents may 'have a healthy commitment to certain goods and an understanding of the limits of markets. Protests reveal neither irrationality nor strategic rationality, but decent ethical commitments' (O'Neill, 1993: 120). Given that the economic valuation of non-human entities is far from the neutral process of commensuration that economists presuppose, their criticisms of those who make an emotive appeal concerning the use of money as a yardstick do not carry force. Economists may (mistakenly) assume their methods to be neutral, but their subjects may balk at the implicit idea of the 'commodification' of particular aspects of the environment (Jacobs, 1994: 80ff.). One explanation of the fact that WTA compensation is frequently significantly higher than WTP is that the former provides a vehicle (though an unsatisfactory one) for the expression of the ethical dimension of the valuation of public goods (Kahnemann and Knetsch, 1992: 69).[17]

Economists are straying into an area where their methodology appears almost meaningless, losing much of its conceptual rigour. Either a strong claim needs to be made that the diversity of values is of purely instrumental significance with respect to the single value of utility maximisation – a claim that we have already argued lacks foundation – or it must be recognised that there are other values aside from utility that cannot be adequately represented by economic valuation techniques. Economists may provide a scale by which different entities can be compared, but this can at best be only an extremely partial representation of the value of any entity. Comparing only such a partial value distorts the particularity of different types of value. As Jack Knetsch argues, 'although CVM studies are almost guaranteed to produce numbers . . . these numbers do not appear to be economic values. While the enthusiasm for valuations may never have been stronger, the evidence that we may indeed be getting misleading answers to the wrong question is pervasive' (Knetsch, 1994: 363).

Allocational efficiency as a decision rule

Even if we were somehow able to overcome these different conceptual problems related to the nature and construction of individual preferences, the use of CBA is also challenged on the grounds that allocational efficiency is given priority as a decision rule to guide decision making. There are a number of related concerns here: whose preferences are to be aggregated; the implications of the Kaldor–Hicks test; and the relative significance of efficiency itself.

In order to ascertain the efficiency of a particular option, individual preferences need to be aggregated. Thus, there is a prior question concerning *whose* preferences are to be taken into account in judgements of efficiency. As Plant contends, the appropriate community of concern is not clear cut:

> to *which* moral community across space and time should the calculation of consequences over interests range? Without some kind of antecedently justified notion of what is the appropriate community of interests, utilitarian calculation lacks determinacy, but it is unclear whether the boundaries of such a moral community could be derived from utilitarianism itself.
>
> (Plant, 1991: 181)[18]

Even if theoretically problematic, the view from the UK Treasury, for example, is clear: 'Costs and benefits should generally be confined to those falling on United Kingdom residents' (HM Treasury, 1997: 20). Environmental values are to be treated in the same way as any costs and benefits associated with the national economy. But the nature of certain environmental values, in particular those recognised (although misrepresented) by environmental economists as 'option' and 'existence' values, again opens up a space to challenge such assumptions.

It is well understood that pollution has transboundary effects on both humans and the wider environment. The Treasury is explicit in recognising that where a project 'is deliberately intended to have cross-border effects' the environmental costs and benefits on non-citizens and other political communities should be included in any analysis (ibid.). However, there are still problems associated with deciding who the relevant affected community should be. For example, in the case of Twyford Down, where an environmentally significant site was to be damaged to make way for the construction of a motorway, whose preferences should count? The drivers who will have a quicker route? The local community who may have less traffic passing through their town but will lose an important cultural landscape? Or, wider still, all those who value such areas? This is where the recognition of values beyond 'actual use' value begins to raise distinct problems for the analyst and the decision maker.

It is far from clear that the community of concern is, or should be, a particular geographically based political community. In the previous chapter, we highlighted the transformative power of certain aspects of the environment to shape our emotions, attitudes and preferences. Such a power may be related to aspects of the environment spatially far away, but proximal to us in the sense that they constitute a significant aspect of our thoughts and actions. One of the most obvious examples is the values that people associate with the rainforests of Borneo, Brazil and the like. Where is the 'cut-off point' for the inclusion of such values in any decision-making process that affects such aspects of the environment? Whose values should count in decision-making processes? Neo-classical economics, and the utilitarian tradition from which it is drawn, has difficulties in answering these questions.

Assuming that this problem of the basis for a decision can be overcome, there are a range of concerns about the decision rule embodied within CBA, i.e. allocational efficiency in the form of potential Pareto optimality. The standing of 'potentiality' within the Kaldor–Hicks test raises practical and ethical challenges. Sen, for example, argues that the compensation criteria within potential Pareto optimality 'are either *unconvincing* or *redundant*': redundant if compensation is in fact paid since the decision can then be said to be Pareto efficient; unconvincing if not paid since this would be ethically questionable – the losers in CBA calculations, Sen argues, are frequently 'the most miserable in society, and it is little consolation to be told that it is possible to compensate them fully, but ("good God!") no actual plans exist to do so' (Sen, 1987: 33). Faced with, for instance, a polluting company, the logic of the Kaldor–Hicks criterion of efficiency would be that pollution should continue as long as the benefits of the production process outweigh the disbenefits to society. 'A Kaldor–Hicks or "potential" Pareto improvement criterion for efficiency would permit the pollution as long as the polluter *could* compensate his victims . . . compensation need not in fact be paid' (Sagoff, 1988: 60; italics added).

The prioritisation of such a principle to guide interventions and policy displays an indifference to other values such as justice and equity. As Williams argues:

> A system of social decision making which is indifferent to issues of justice or equity certainly has less to worry about than one that is not indifferent to those considerations. But that type of minimal commitment is enticing. The desirability of a system of social

choice can be considered only relative to what it can reasonably asked to do, and the simplicity of utilitarianism in this respect is no virtue if it fails to do what can be reasonably required of government, as for instance to consider issues of equity. Certainly the simplicity that utilitarianism can acquire from neglecting these demands is not itself an argument for saying that the demands should be met.

(Williams, 1973b: 137)

The principle of allocational efficiency is enshrined within CBA through the use of potential Pareto optimality (the Kaldor–Hicks compensation test) as the single criterion of preference aggregation. Comparisons between policy options are purely comparisons of allocational efficiency: given a particular state of affairs, what is the most efficient allocation of goods? But why should efficiency have ascendancy over other criteria such as justice or equality? This is a particularly pertinent question given our earlier support for value pluralism in the previous chapter.

The prioritisation of allocational efficiency results in a disposition towards policy options that generate the highest NPV, to the neglect of other values. This is seen as a contribution to the expansion of the economy. As the then UK Department of Transport (DOT) stated in its defence of large-scale road schemes: 'The resulting 'Net Present Value' (NPV) measures the contribution the scheme makes to national economic benefits. . . which feed into higher GDP' (DOT, 1991: 5).[19] In the case of road building, a focus on NPV generally favours high cost over smaller schemes which tend to 'manage' traffic. Absolute return of costs over benefits typically sway decision makers: 'public policy has been dominated by concerns over 'value for money' in public expenditure. In this context a measure that purports to show cash returns from public investment has a greater influence on decision-makers' (Atkins, 1990: 7). Efficiency and maximisation of output come to dominate policy decisions with detrimental effects on other desiderata such as equity.[20] As Charles Taylor argues:

The fear is that things that ought to be determined by other criteria will be decided in terms of efficiency or 'cost–benefit' analysis, that the independent ends that ought to be guiding our lives will be eclipsed by the demand to maximise output. There are lots of things one can point to that give substance to this worry: for instance, the ways that demands of economic growth are used to justify very unequal distributions of wealth and income, or the way these demands make us insensitive to the needs of the environment, even to the point of potential disaster.

(Taylor, 1992: 5–6)

This prioritisation of efficiency finds a comfortable home among advocates of ecological modernisation. The logic of 'environmentally sensitive' allocational efficiency is at the heart of this dominant interpretation of sustainable development, which holds that, once environmental externalities have been internalised, environmental sustainability can be promoted through eco-efficiency – the efficient use of natural resources. As was briefly discussed in the Introduction, ecological modernisation takes a particular stance on the question of economy–environment integration, stressing the importance of the environmental *efficiency* of the economy. But ecological modernisation comes at a price, and at least two of its weaknesses are mirrored within the use of CBA.[21] First, the focus on eco-efficiency or environmentally sensitive allocational efficiency means that other values, in particular social justice, are not addressed. Both social justice *within* industrialised nations and *between* nations, in particular between highly industrialised and Third World nations, are ignored. Thus, it is 'more efficient' to site toxic waste disposal sites closer to lower socioeconomic neighbourhoods or export polluting industries and to degrade environmental resources in less industrialised nations. Ecological modernisation fails to engage with the social contradictions of capitalism (Hajer, 1995: 32). Second, both ecological modernisation and the economic valuation of the environment fail to adequately address the plurality of 'non-instrumental' values associated with the environment. Valuation techniques such as CV allow for the integration of the (total) economic value of non-human nature within decision-making processes; the environment is no longer viewed as a free good. However, this remains a highly instrumental view of nature. Within ecological modernisation, a reorientation towards the natural world is promoted for reasons of efficiency and not for ethical reasons. Environmental impacts are internalised, but only in economic terms. And, as we have already argued, such internalisation misrepresents the different types of value that we associate with the non-human world and erodes an ecologically sensitive understanding of anthropocentrism.

CBA privileges allocational efficiency. But there is no reason why efficiency should always take priority. Institutions could be designed such that a full range of alternative basis for judgement can be offered and assessed. Efficiency needs to take its place alongside other values and possible decision rules, such as equity, or perhaps even the contested deep ecological 'land ethic' or 'biospherical egalitarianism'.[22] Individual and collective judgements are made in relation to a variety of different values which may well conflict. The institutional setting for decision making needs to be sensitive to the incommensurability and incompatibility between values.

The pragmatic defence of cost–benefit analysis

The critique of economic valuation of the environment and the use of extended CBA has followed two broad trajectories: first, an argument that individual preferences incorporate ethical judgements and that different types of values are not commensurable with or reducible to a single monetary value; and, second, an argument that questions the priority given to allocational efficiency as a decision rule. Some economists recognise that their techniques may be far from perfect but offer an additional pragmatic defence of economic valuation:

> economic (monetary) valuation of non-market environmental assets may be more or less imperfect given the particular asset together with its environmental and valuation contexts; but, invariably, some valuation explicitly laid out for scrutiny by policy-makers and the public, is better than none, because none can mean some implicit valuation shrouded from public scrutiny.
>
> (Turner *et al*, 1994: 109)

This pragmatic argument has tempted a number of greens to offer their qualified support for CBA, but it needs to be challenged. Kerry Turner and his colleagues state that valuations are 'explicitly laid out for scrutiny'. However, a CBA is typically a whole series of figures in two rows of costs and benefits totalled into a NPV. Individuals' preferences are incorporated into these calculations, but the judgements and techniques used by economists to generate these figures are 'shrouded from public scrutiny'. Any sense of transparency is lost. The economist has privileged access to the process. Faced by such an array of figures, decision makers and the public are, typically, drawn to the relative size of NPVs. On the rare occasions on which decisions are subject to public challenge in the UK, for example, in public inquiries for road building, inspectors have typically ruled challenges to the use of CBA illegitimate: objectors 'have been told that it is government policy to rely on ... CBA ... in making decisions about new roads, and that scrutiny of government policy is the business of Parliament' (Adams, 1995: 1).

Why careful public scrutiny is required becomes obvious if we briefly focus on the use of CBA in road building. This is, after all, a controversial area of public policy, which sparked some of the most intense environmental direct action in UK history (Wall, 1999; Seel *et al.*, 2000; Connelly and Smith, 2003). Individual schemes in *Roads for Prosperity* (DOT, 1989) were not subject to the extended form of CBA argued for by environmental economists, but analysis of the valuations included within the DOT's CBA process (known as COBA) highlights the type of contentious judgements that can justify highly destructive policy decisions.[23]

Calculations of time savings are the dominant benefits of any trunk road proposal and represent the foremost quantification of the then DOT's policy objective 'to assist economic growth by reducing transport costs' (DOT, 1989: 4; 1992: 20): 'Typically, time savings account for 85% to 90% of the gross benefits of a trunk road scheme' (DOT, 1991: 5). These calculations of time savings expose two associated methodological problems with the CBA process: first, the incorporation of individual preferences based on behaviour; and, second, the aggregation of these individual preferences.

Using economic valuation techniques, the DOT assigned a figure of 153.2 pence per hour per person for non-working time journeys (at 1985 prices) (DOT, 1987: 5). The first problem is that the time saving valuation within COBA has no regard for those individuals who have strong environmental commitments and may have been prepared to accept a longer journey time in the knowledge that a sensitive landscape such as Twyford Down was being conserved. Behaviour is equated to commitment. As Stephen Atkins writes, 'The likelihood is that many people find that their short-term travel behaviour choices are being used to justify decisions that they would not support "politically"' (Atkins, 1990: 8). Simply because they use a stretch of road, it is assumed that all drivers will prefer a quicker journey. Second, there is a problem of aggregating small increments of time such that benefits of £100 million or more are apparently achieved. It is assumed in economic analysis that an individual accords the same value to a large time period as to the equivalent aggregation of small time periods. If, for instance, an individual saves one minute every day using a proposed road scheme in non-working time, it is assumed that the aggregation of those small daily savings is valued in the same way as a single period of six hours. Outside of the limited assumptions of neo-classical economic theory, it is questionable as to whether such small time savings are even noticed and, even if they are, whether they are of any productive use compared with the longer time span to which they are apparently equivalent. In 1990, the House of Commons Transport Select Committee argued: 'The assumption that small increments of time have real economic value when aggregated over a large number of vehicles is unsubstantiated' (quoted in Bray, 1995: 9). When the aggregation of time savings is commonly in the range of £100 million and is the principle quantified benefit of a scheme, the cogency of such assumptions needs to be challenged. But there is no political space in which such challenges can take place.

Perhaps of even more concern than the dubious methodological implications of time savings is the figure placed on the value of life used to assess the changing safety costs and benefits. Without getting embroiled in ethical questions concerning the economic value of a statistical life (VOSL), it highlights how politically motivated values are 'shrouded from public scrutiny' within CBA. Originally the DOT used a human capital approach to assess VOSL which in 1987 equated to £252,500 (1985 prices): 'Under current practice, a major constituent of that value is an estimate of the gross contribution to GDP that an accident victim would otherwise have made had death or injury not occurred. The value also includes an estimate of medical costs and a subjectively assessed addition for pain, grief and suffering' (DOT, 1987: 6). This approach was controversial and, facing widespread criticism, the DOT instigated further research (Jones-Lee, 1985; 1990; Dalvi, 1988). An analysis of the levels used in other OECD countries, CV studies and hedonic and wage differential approaches concluded that the VOSL was a serious underestimate and placed the value close to £2 million. Even in light of the results of their own research, the DOT raised the value to only £635,180 (1991 prices). If the value had been raised higher it 'would probably change the present relationship between time savings and accident benefits and would relatively downgrade the priority given to faster traffic movement and congestion as opposed to safety of life and limb' (Dalvi, quoted in Barde and Pearce, 1991: 230). As the DOT stated: 'the choice of a value is essentially a political assessment of the balance to be struck between mobility and safety' (DOT, 1987: 7). The debates over VOSL expose not only the differential results obtained from the variety of economic valuation techniques, but also that explicitly *political* judgements are being imputed into CBAs.

The UK Treasury's 'The Green Book' explicitly uses 'the valuation of working and of leisure time in the calculation of costs and benefits of a road scheme' as its example of the way that non-market impacts can be valued 'in ways which are widely enough accepted to be used as a basis for policy decisions' (HM Treasury, 1991: 45). But, both this valuation and the VOSL are highly contentious and the claim by the Treasury that they are 'widely accepted' and by Turner and his colleagues that they are 'explicitly laid out for scrutiny by policy-makers and the public' are controversial at best.[24] The nature of valuations in CBAs are far from explicit, and it is the judgements of economists and the political decisions of policy makers that are actually 'shrouded from public scrutiny' within the process. The expert authority of economists and the political assumptions inherent within economic valuation and the CBA procedure are not open to challenge. If this is the case with more established areas of economic analysis, any extension into more detailed environmental valuation will be even more controversial. Some greens may be tempted to support extended-CBA on the grounds that, on occasion, economic valuation of environmental goods might halt environmentally-destructive projects. However, rather than extending a procedure that will grossly distort the plurality of values that we associate with the environment, surely the limits of economic techniques need to be recognised and more suitable institutional mechanisms sought.

Lessons for institutional design

Cost–benefit analysis is one of the more sophisticated techniques used within liberal democratic institutions to aggregate individuals' preferences into a collective choice. If the use of CBA misrepresents environmental values, then it is implicit that greens (and others) need to offer alternative designs for decision making, approaches that are more sensitive to the plurality of environmental (and other) values. The remainder of this chapter will briefly dwell on some of the lessons that might be drawn from the weaknesses of CBA.

CBA is an excellent example of an aggregation technique that prioritises allocational efficiency. But, according to value pluralism, efficiency is just one of a diversity of values that might guide policy decisions. Conditions need to be created in political institutions in which a diversity of what may be incommensurable and incompatible values, goods or decision rules in judgements can be appealed to, and the alternative policy options that emerge assessed.

Prior to aggregation, individual judgements are sought. The form that these judgements take is a further matter of concern. First, the utilitarian framework that is the basis of CBA takes preferences as being given and incorrigible (Plant, 1991: 140). Preference formation is assumed to be exogenous, with economic techniques simply 'revealing' pre-existing preference. But evidence from the practice of CV itself shows that this is not the case. Respondents' valuations are affected by, for example, the type of information made available, the initial bids offered by interviewers and the vehicle of payment. More broadly, aggregation processes such as CBA fail to recognise that preferences, interests and values are shaped and constrained by the political, social and economic context in which individuals find themselves: numerous social forces shape an individual's sense of what is possible. As Cass Sunstein has argued, poverty 'is perhaps the most severe obstacle to the free development of preferences and beliefs' (Sunstein, 1991: 23). Preferences are not exogenous to social and institutional settings: 'preferences are not fixed and stable, but are instead adaptive to a wide range of factors . . . The phenomenon of endogenous preferences casts doubt on the notion that a democratic government ought to respect private desires and beliefs in all or almost all contexts' (ibid.: 5). Hence, decision-making procedures should be concerned not only with aggregating preferences, but also with the nature of the processes through which they are *formed*.

This takes us naturally to the second problem with the way that CBA deals with individual judgements: the assumption that they can be understood as judgements about utility maximisation. If judgements were of this type, then we might be unconcerned that individuals make their valuations in CV processes in isolation. Judgement would be a private affair. But we have already argued that judgements about the environment will reflect various ethical commitments. In Chapter 1, we made the case that such judgements require the development of an enlarged mentality, which is itself dependent on reflection on the judgements of others. This suggests the need for dialogue between citizens to promote such reflection and consideration of their own and others' values and preferences. The privatisation of judgement undermines the consideration of differing perspectives and value orientations and thus inhibits the exercise of judgement. All institutions shape how judgements are made. But the institutions of liberal democracies are typically not designed to encourage engagement and the testing of preferences and value orientations.

Finally, the use of CBA throws up a concern about the exercise of both political and expert authority in decision-making processes. Currently, economists have a privileged position within decision-making procedures: they are responsible for converting individual preferences into a calculable form. Even if an extended form of CBA that includes environmental valuations is not used, more limited forms of CBA are likely to continue to be part of decision making. Similarly, other experts, such as scientists, engineers and academics will play a role. The significance of their expert status needs to be considered since decisions affecting the environment will need to weigh evidence from a variety of sources, evidence that is likely to be contested.

Conclusion

CBA is a technique that is increasingly used within contemporary political institutions as a way of including the values of citizens in the assessment of environmental policy. That the opinions of citizens should be sought is not questioned; whether CBA provides an accurate reflection of values and preferences is, however, in doubt. If we are to be sensitive to the plurality of values we associate with the environment, appropriate institutional settings and contexts need to be designed, in which these values can be articulated and reflected on without attempting to transform or manipulate them into a form that misrepresents their distinctive characteristics. For greens, opportunities must be available within political institutions to articulate their concerns and challenge perspectives which lack sensitivity to environmental values The rest of this book takes as its task the analysis of an alternative approach to developing institutions that are able to effectively reflect the plurality of values we associate with the environment. This analysis begins with the emerging literature on deliberative democracy.

3 Deliberative democracy and green political theory

Contemporary liberal democratic institutions are charged with lacking sensitivity to the plurality of values we associate with the non-human world, and with employing techniques to guide decision making, in particular cost–benefit analysis (CBA), that misrepresent and distort the nature of environmental values. How might we begin to reform and restructure political institutions so that they are more sensitive to environmental considerations? Theories of deliberative democracy offer an interesting theoretical response to this question: they promise institutions that promote democratic deliberation (inclusive and reasoned political dialogue), which will be sensitive to the plurality of environmental values and which will promote political judgement that takes into consideration different perspectives on the non-human world.

This chapter begins with a summary of recent work on deliberative democracy, highlighting the importance of inclusiveness and unconstrained dialogue in the political process. Given that deliberative democracy has established itself as a new orthodoxy within contemporary democratic theory, it should be no surprise that it has been the subject of much debate within green political theory. The chapter offers a number of arguments as to why greens should support the enhancement of democratic deliberation, and considers some of the challenges raised by sympathetic critics. Although there can be no guarantee of green policy outcomes, deliberative democracy offers conditions under which the plurality of environmental (and other) values can be articulated and considered. However, it is accepted that it is a fair criticism that the literature on deliberative democracy remains highly abstract and theoretical: the chapter ends with some initial thoughts on the institutionalisation of democratic deliberation.

Deliberative democracy

The growing interest in forms of deliberative democracy indicates, on the one hand, a widespread dissatisfaction with aspects of our contemporary political practices and, on the other hand, a reflective awareness that alternative practices are plausible options for us.[1] Within contemporary democratic theory, there is an emerging concern with the growing difference and distance between the subjectivity, motives and intentions of citizens and the political decisions made in their name (e.g. Barber, 1984; Offe and Preuss, 1991; Phillips, 1995). For many critics, the activities, backgrounds and interests of political representatives and decision makers are seen as far removed from the lives and perspectives of citizens. Although periodic elections act as 'a continuous discipline on the elected to take constant notice of public opinion' (Beetham, 1992: 47), the mandate that representatives enjoy extends over a period during which time citizens have very little impact on decisions made in their name. The principal-agent form of representation, so dominant within liberal democracies, rests on the fact that the political representative is able to deliberate and decide *for* others (Pitkin, 1967: 42–3). But critics contend that the influence of party interests and lack of presence or 'voice' of the politically marginalised in political decision-making processes means that their interests and perspectives are systematically excluded, or at least not adequately addressed. As Anne Phillips argues, 'when policies are worked out *for* rather than *with* a politically excluded constituency, they are unlikely to engage all relevant concerns' (Phillips, 1995: 13). The plurality of environmental values and the interests of 'environmental constituencies' – contemporary non-nationals, future generations and non-human nature (Eckersley, 1996: 214; Dobson, 1996a: 124) – are poorly represented in the deliberations and decisions of liberal democratic institutions.

Clearly, the political activity and influence of citizens extends beyond voting, and contemporary society is marked by a plurality of interest groups and associations. However, the democratic nature of this pluralism is undermined by the social and economic imbalances inherent within society. Expressions of economic power and social influence undermine, to a large extent, the assumption of political equality on which liberal representative institutions are frequently defended (Arblaster, 1987: 76). As David Beetham argues: 'The freedoms of speech and association not only provide the guarantee of a more extensive political activity than the vote; they are also the means whereby the inequalities of civil society are transmitted to the political domain' (Beetham, 1992: 48).

Given the inequality inherent within civil society and political institutions, to what extent can widely used social choice mechanisms, such as voting, CBA, opinion polling and the market, be viewed as neutral? Do these conditions undermine the influential liberal principle that the role of democracy is to aggregate individuals' pre-given preferences into a collective choice (Miller, 1992: 54; Phillips, 1995: 149)? Our analysis of CBA in the previous chapter highlighted that such social choice mechanisms are frequently subject to strategic manipulation (Miller, 1992: 59) and ignore the influence of institutions on the shaping of preferences. By taking preferences as given and incorrigible, aggregation techniques such as CBA fail to recognise that preferences, interests and values are shaped and constrained by the political, social and economic context in which individuals find themselves. Preferences are not exogenous to institutional settings: decision-making procedures should be concerned not only with aggregating preferences, but also with the nature of the processes through which they are *formed* (Sunstein, 1991). However, contemporary liberal institutions are not designed to encourage engagement and the testing of preferences and value orientations (Warren, 1996a: 242) – citizenship is typically a passive affair which, it is argued, leads to 'a moral and political "de-skilling" of the electorate and the spread of cynical attitudes about public affairs and the notion of a public good' (Offe and Preuss, 1991: 165).

Given the lack of critical engagement on the part of citizens, the danger is that political elites are not 'effectively called upon to comply to demanding standards of political rationality and responsibility' (ibid.: 165). In such a climate, the very legitimacy of liberal forms of political authority, grounded on the neutrality of procedures, is challenged. As Mark Warren argues:

> rules and procedures always have normative purposes, and the authority they carry depends on these. They are never neutral, and our decision to abide by them cannot be neutral. We hold rules as

authoritative (or lacking in authority) because of the normatively significant work they do. If the rules and procedures produce normatively questionable outcomes, then they tend to lose their authority

(Warren, 1996b: 55)

Deliberative democratic theory has evolved in response to the perceived weaknesses of liberal democratic theory and practice and offers a challenge to, and a critical perspective from which to judge, the institutions of contemporary liberal democratic states. Although there is a recognition that a division of political labour is necessary, given the complexity of contemporary political, economic and social conditions, deliberative democracy offers the possibility of a different *form* of that division, one in which increased opportunities for citizen engagement are taken to be both feasible and desirable, and in which citizen engagement forms part of an ongoing critical dialogue upon which more legitimate forms of political authority can be grounded.[2] As Seyla Benhabib argues:

> According to the deliberative model of democracy, it is a necessary condition for attaining legitimacy and rationality with regard to collective decision-making processes in a polity, that the institutions in this polity are so arranged that what is considered in the common interest of all results from processes of collective deliberation conducted rationally and fairly among free and equal individuals.
>
> (Benhabib, 1996: 69)

Deliberative democracy shares with liberal theories the desire to create political institutions that will resolve conflict, but it recognises that in the *process* of engagement individuals' preferences and value orientations can be transformed (Miller, 1992; Phillips, 1995).[3] Thus, the context of engagement takes on profound significance. According to theories of deliberative democracy, two fundamental conditions need to be fulfilled for the emergence of more legitimate and trustworthy forms of political authority: inclusiveness and unconstrained dialogue.

Inclusiveness relates to both presence and voice: in principle, all citizens are entitled to participate in the process of political dialogue and have an equal right to introduce and question claims, to put forward reasons, to express and challenge needs, values and interests.[4] Voices should not be excluded from the political process; citizens have an equal right to be heard.

Unconstrained dialogue requires the promotion of 'deliberative' as opposed to 'strategic' or 'instrumental' rationality. In contrast to the strategic manipulation and manoeuvring that is often characteristic of contemporary politics, we can describe a collective as *deliberatively* rational 'to the extent that its interactions are egalitarian, uncoerced, competent, and free from delusion, deception, power and strategy' (Dryzek, 1990a: 202).[5] Sympathetic feminist theorists, in particular Iris Marion Young, have raised concerns that some conceptions of democratic dialogue may be too narrowly restricted to a particularly rigid form and style of rational argumentation: 'polite, orderly, dispassionate, gentlemanly argument' (Young, 2000: 49). The privileging of a specific type of debate and expression may have the effect of silencing antagonisms and contestation and devaluing the perspectives of those who are less skilled in such forms of argument.[6] Young proposes that a richer and broader conception of deliberative democracy requires not only critical argument, but also greeting, rhetoric, and narrative or storytelling (Young, 1996: 128–33; 2000: 53–80).[7]

> Greeting, or in political contexts public acknowledgement, is a form of communication where a subject recognises the subjectivity of others, thereby fostering trust. Rhetoric, the ways the political assertions and arguments are expressed, has several functions that contribute to inclusive and persuasive political communication, including calling attention to points and situating speakers and audience in relation to one another. Narrative also has several functions that counter exclusive tendencies and further argument. Among other functions, narrative empowers relatively disenfranchised groups to assert themselves publicly; it also offers means by which people whose experiences and beliefs differ so much that they do not share enough premises to engage in fruitful debate can nevertheless reach dialogical understanding.
>
> (Young, 2000: 53)

This broadening of what is understood as legitimate forms of communication is important, especially if all voices are to be heard and considered. However, whatever form deliberations take, it is fundamental that they are non-coercive and are orientated towards broadening the understanding and perspectives of participants. Just as rational argument can be used to manipulate and deceive, so too can these other forms of communication (ibid.: 77–80). Deliberative institutions need to be alive to, and protect against, strategic and manipulative actions.

Taken together, inclusiveness and unconstrained dialogue offer the basis for more legitimate and trustworthy forms of political authority. As Bernard Manin contends, it is 'necessary to alter radically the perspective common to both liberal theories and democratic thought: the source of legitimacy is not the predetermined will of individuals, but rather the process of its formation, that is deliberation itself' (Manin, 1987: 351–2). Along similar lines, Amy Gutmann argues: 'the legitimate exercise of political authority requires justification to those people who are bound by it, and decision-making by deliberation among free and equal citizens is the most defensible justification anyone has to offer for provisionally settling controversial issues' (Gutmann, 1996: 344). Democratic legitimacy and trust in authority is generated by an ongoing context of critical scrutiny and opportunities for discursive challenge (Warren, 1996a: 55).

Although the legitimacy of decisions and institutional arrangements rests on achieving inclusiveness and unconstrained dialogue, there is no account provided here of how decisions are to be made. This is a controversial and yet relatively under-theorised issue within deliberative democratic theory, and we will have reason to return to it on a number of occasions. At this point in the argument, it is necessary to deal with the status of 'consensus' in deliberative democratic theory. For many, consensus is the regulative ideal or implicit standard of democratic dialogue (Cohen, 1989: 23; Eriksen, 2000: 62). Theorists who place emphasis on the achievement of consensus are typically heavily influenced by Jürgen Habermas's argument that consensus on moral norms is implicit within the very structure of speech acts (Habermas, 1990; 1993).[8] Although an orientation towards consensus may be an admirable goal, there are practical concerns about its role in actual political discourse. The account of value pluralism offered in Chapter 1 – in particular the recognition that conflicting values may well be incommensurable and/or incompatible – raises the spectre that consensus may simply not be achievable for complex policy decisions. Value pluralism, and the ensuing conflict and indeterminacy in moral and political debate, undermines a strong commitment to, or expectation of, consensus. Additionally, concerns have been raised that an expectation of consensus can create a barrier to critical dialogue and lead to further marginalisation of disadvantaged groups and perspectives: 'the perspectives of the privileged are likely to dominate the definition of the common good' (Young, 1996: 126; also Mansbridge, 1983). The assumption of unanimity and consensus may mean that members of a dominant culture or those in a majority on particular issues see no reason to test and/or revise their perspectives to account for alternative experiences, knowledge and insights.

Rather than consensus, democratic deliberation is best understood as being orientated towards *mutual understanding*, which does not mean that people will always agree, 'but rather that they are motivated to resolve conflicts by argument rather than other means' (Warren, 1995: 181; also Chambers, 1995: 237). An emphasis on mutual understanding highlights the requirement on participants to confront the variety of points of view on particular issues and to be open to the possibility of the transformation of preferences after reflection on, and consideration of, their own and others' perspectives (Baynes, 1995: 216; Manin, 1987: 351). It requires that citizens recognise the limitations and fallibility of their own perspectives and judgements. In this light, value pluralism and the 'difference' embodied within perspectives can be considered as a 'resource' for democracy rather than as something to be overcome. It is only through encountering other perspectives and value orientations that we are able to reflect upon and transform our own perspectives and come to more reasoned judgements (Young, 1996: 126–8). As Jeremy Waldron argues, deliberation 'is a way of bringing each citizen's ethical views and insights – such as they are – to bear on each other, providing a basis for reciprocal questioning and criticism and enabling a view to emerge which is better than any of the inputs and much more than the mere aggregation or function of those inputs' (Waldron, 1999: 106). Aggregation techniques such as CBA tend to priviledge private preferences and judgements rather than encourage mutual understanding.

However, such openness to the perspectives of others is not guaranteed by simply establishing rules of inclusiveness and non-coercion in dialogue. Citizens need to cultivate a particular disposition: internal attitudes of mutual respect and impartiality (Chambers, 1995: 340) that allow the development of imagination and empathy. It requires citizens to take other perspectives seriously; to afford them an equal right to moral authority; to cultivate a disposition towards openness such that they reflect on their own values and preferences in light of conflicting perspectives; and, finally, to avoid unnecessary conflict in order to keep the political dialogue open and in recognition of the possibility of further transformation (Gutmann and Thompson, 1990: 79–82).[9] Thus, democratic deliberation requires a form of judgement as 'enlarged mentality', which we initially discussed in Chapter 1 (Arendt, 1968; 1982).

The development of enlarged mentality entails a degree of moral courage to appreciate and acknowledge the force of arguments offered by people with whom we disagree. For those in the majority on a particular policy, it requires the cultivation of the virtue of civic responsiveness, a willingness to listen to and reflect upon the perspectives of those in the minority. And for those in the minority, it requires the cultivation of civic endurance, the continuing and ongoing motivation to persuade others of the veracity and significance of their particular perspectives (Bentley and Owen, 2001).

Mutual understanding grounds democratic legitimacy, but without the excessive requirement of consensus. Legitimacy rests on all participants understanding and accepting how and why a particular outcome was reached, even if disagreement remains about the substantive nature of any decision (Miller, 2002). Thus, political decisions might arise from, for example, the (occasional) emergence of consensus, workable agreement based on competing reasons and commitments, compromise and majority–minority decisions. As long as participants accept the conditions under which collective decisions and judgements are reached, disagreement does not undermine deliberation. In societies characterised by value pluralism, we need to recognise that antagonisms and contestations will exist across a wide range of policy issues and cannot be theorised away (Moon, 1995; Waldron, 1999).

Implicit within deliberative democracy is an active conception of citizenship. There is an emphasis on citizens cultivating empathy and acknowledging different and often conflicting perspectives and forms of reasoning. This again highlights why the aggregation of individual private judgements (as in CBA) is deeply suspect in *political* decision making. As Warren argues:

> democracy works poorly when individuals hold preferences and make judgements in isolation from one another, as they often do in today's liberal democracies. When individuals lack the opportunities, incentives, and necessities to test, articulate, defend, and ultimately act on their judgements, they will also be lacking in empathy for others, poor in information, and unlikely to have the critical skills necessary to articulate, defend, and revise their views.
>
> (Warren, 1996b: 242)

Deliberative democracy promises much: more trustworthy and legitimate forms of political authority based on inclusive and unconstrained dialogue, more informed political judgements and decisions, and a more active account of citizenship. It promises a political environment within which the plurality of environmental values can be effectively and sensitively assessed and considered in decision-making processes.

Green politics and deliberative democracy

Just as deliberative democracy is fast establishing itself as a new orthodoxy within contemporary democratic theory, it is having a similar impact within green political thought. A roll-call of prominent green theorists would highlight a significant level of commitment to the deliberative democratic ideal.[10]

The earliest and best-known advocate of deliberative democracy from within green politics is John Dryzek. In a number of works, he has stressed that deliberative institutions are likely to be more 'ecologically rational' than other social choice mechanisms, including liberal democratic institutions, in that they have the ability to respond to the high levels of complexity, uncertainty and collective action problems associated with many contemporary environmental problems (Dryzek, 1987). According to Dryzek, the ability of a political mechanism to incorporate negative feedback and coordination is a necessary condition for ecological rationality (ibid.: 54). Negative feedback is 'the ability to generate corrective movement when a natural system's equilibrium is disturbed'; while coordination refers to both coordination *across different problems* 'so that solving a problem in one place does not simply create greater problems elsewhere' and coordination *across actors* 'to supply public goods or prevent the tragedy of the commons' (Dryzek, 1995: 16).

Dryzek's arguments refer to the ability of democratic deliberation to lessen the problem of bounded rationality: 'the fact that our imaginations and calculating abilities are limited and fallible' (Fearon, 1998: 49; also Torgerson, 1999). Deliberation offers the conditions under which actors can widen their own limited and fallible perspectives by drawing on each other's knowledge, experience and capabilities. James Fearon argues that this increases the odds of good judgements emerging for two reasons: it might be 'additively' valuable in the sense that one actor is able to offer an analysis or solution that had not occurred to others; or it might be 'multiplicatively' valuable in that deliberation could lead to solutions that would not have occurred to the participants individually (ibid.: 50).

Theoretically, democratic deliberation improves information flow by actively engaging numerous voices, including those individuals and groups with direct experience of the effects of environmental change. Too often, decision makers in liberal democracies are far removed from the impact of their decisions, and the experiences, knowledge and perspectives of those whose practices are more attuned to the changes in ecosystems are not articulated. Knowledge is dispersed (Fischer, 2000). Similarly, deliberative institutional arrangements are more likely to overcome coordination problems. Here, Dryzek draws on the widely accepted experimental evidence in game theory which suggests that a period of discussion between participants *prior* to making choices markedly promotes 'cooperative' over 'defecting' strategies and thus goes some way to overcoming the collective action problems that are at the heart of many environmental problems, in particular the underprovision of public goods (Dryzek, 1987: 211).

Dryzek's pragmatic epistemological arguments about ecological rationality are, for politically expedient reasons, restricted to a minimal, instrumental conception of environmental values.[11] Because he is attempting to identify a *generalisable* principle of respect for particular aspects of nature that is logically prior to all other competing normative principles, the conception of ecological rationality is restricted to 'only the productive, protective and waste-assimilative value of ecosystems – that is, those aspects which provide the basic requirements for human life' (Dryzek, 1987: 34).[12] However, beyond such a circumscribed understanding of the value of the environment, deliberative democracy offers a conducive environment in which the plurality of environmental and other values can be articulated and explored in the development of public policy.

Democratic deliberation encourages mutual recognition and respect and is orientated toward shared understanding and the public recognition of the common good. Given the disparate nature of the green movement and the plurality of environmental (and other) values which are often incommensurable, and at times conflict (see Chapter 1), democratic deliberation offers appropriate conditions under which such tensions can be understood and explored. Democratic deliberation promises much in that it provides motivation and encouragement to articulate preferences and justifications which are 'public-spirited' in nature. David Miller stresses the 'moralising effect of public discussion': the reciprocal requirement to put forward reasons and to respond to challenges will tend to eliminate irrational preferences based on false empirical beliefs, morally repugnant preferences that no one is willing to advance in the public arena, and narrowly self-regarding preferences (Miller, 1992: 61). The orientation towards the common good means that preferences held on purely self-interested grounds become difficult to defend in a deliberative context: 'we have good reason to expect the deliberative process to transform initial policy preferences (which may be based on private interest, sectional interest, prejudice and so on) into ethical judgements on the matter in hand' (ibid: 62). For greens, the moralising effect of deliberation offers the opportunity to emphasise the ethical nature of human–non-human relations and the public good character of many environmental problems, and to expose and challenge the narrowly self-interested grounds of many environmentally degrading and unsustainable practices.

Greens should also be supportive of sympathetic critics of deliberative democracy who stress the variety of forms of communication (Young, 1996; 2000; Sanders, 1997). The narrative form, for example, is particularly germane for expressing the value of particular landscapes. Through narrative, the sense of place can be evoked such that those who do not share that relationship with the non-human world might come to an understanding of the experience and the values of the narrator. Young offers the example of the manner in which the Lakota use myth to 'convey to others in South Dakota why the Black Hills mean so much to them, and why they believe they have special moral warrant to demand a stop to forestry in the Black Hills . . . . Through narrative the outsiders may come to understand why the insiders value what they value and why they have the priorities they have' (Young, 1996: 132). The poetic imagination expressed through myths and stories can play an important role in expressing relationships with the natural world and allowing people to appreciate perspectives that might otherwise have not been recognised or understood.[13]

Value pluralism cannot be overcome, but deliberation provides an effective context within which enlarged mentality can be cultivated. Ongoing democratic dialogue enhances reflection on the plurality of environmental values and provides the potential for the transformation of perspectives. Robert Goodin has argued that deliberative democratic arrangements offer the most likely mechanism through which people can be induced to internalise nature's interests. Greens (who have already incorporated nature's interests) will have a voice to challenge environmentally insensitive decisions and offer alternative proposals. Further, the public-spirited character of deliberation means that there is also likely to be 'anticipatory internalisation' of green ethical arguments by participants: 'discursive democracy . . . creates a situation in which interests other than your own are called to mind' (Goodin, 1996: 847).[14]

The cultivation of enlarged mentality is fundamental to conceptions of ecological citizenship, the development of an ecological ethos (Torgerson, 1999) and the practice of ecological stewardship (Barry, 1999). It is not simply participation per se that is important to an expression of such democratic citizenship, rather it is a particular form of civic engagement that encourages the public articulation, defence and revision of judgements (Warren, 1996b: 242). Democratic deliberation offers conditions under which citizens will encounter and reflect upon ecological knowledge and values and will be more likely to internalise these in their judgements and practices (Barry, 1999; Goodin, 1996). According to Peter Christoff, such internalisation and social learning can profoundly reshape the boundaries of traditional political citizenship beyond the nation state, generating 'additional and occasionally alternative transnational allegiances ranging from the bio-regional through to the global, as well as to other species and the survival of ecosystems' (Christoff, 1996b: 159). Deliberative processes provide a conducive arena in which citizens can be exposed to alternative ways of conceptualising relations between human and non-human worlds. As Robyn Eckersley argues: 'Public spirited deliberation is the process by which we learn of our dependence on others (and the environment) and the process by which we learn to recognise and respect differently situated others (including non-human others and future generations)' (Eckersley, 2000: 120). Adolf Gundersen offers some initial evidence that deliberation on ecological issues can have a transformative effect on citizens' worldviews, enhancing their support for collective action, as well as leading to more holistic and long-term thinking – all central to the realisation of a more environmentally rational politics (Gundersen, 1995).[15]

The inclusive and deliberative nature of democratic dialogue generates the grounds for more legitimate and trustworthy forms of authority – political and expert – in environmental policy making. The legitimacy of both forms of authority is enhanced by an ongoing context of critical scrutiny and opportunities for discursive challenge (Warren, 1996a). We have already argued that, in contemporary democracies, the formal avenues for citizen engagement in the political process are limited. If political decisions fail to reflect the plurality of environmental values expressed by citizens, then the legitimacy of those in political authority becomes a subject of concern. Critical scrutiny is also crucial for the legitimate exercise of expert forms of authority within political institutions. The analysis of the use of CBA in Chapter 2 raised concerns about the privileged status given to economists in the policy process and the lack of opportunities to challenge the manner in which their 'expert' discourse (mis)represents environmental values. Similar concerns have been raised about the often unchallenged role of expertise in the application of scientific and technological knowledge (Wynne, 1996; Fischer, 2000). Deliberative democracy offers the context within which ongoing discursive engagement and challenge can take place. When faced with high levels of uncertainty and risk, deliberative institutions promise an ingenious mechanism through which the application of scientific and technological knowledge and expertise might be democratically regulated – an institutional setting within which the barriers between 'expert' and 'lay' knowledge can be challenged and reformulated (Beck, 1992; Barry, 1999).

Deliberative democracy is thus of interest to greens for a number of reasons. It offers a conducive environment within which citizens can reflect on knowledge about ecological systems and the plurality of environmental values derived from a variety of different perspectives. The presence of these different perspectives offers the opportunity for the exercise of judgement based on enlarged mentality, whereby competing evidence and incommensurable and incompatible value orientations can be considered. From such a process, more legitimate political decisions can emerge, their legitimacy having been enhanced by reflection and judgement on competing environmental values and perspectives. And the same process of critical engagement also offers a more sustainable basis for the role of expertise in policy formulation. In principle, then, deliberative democracy offers much to green political theory.

The green challenge to deliberative democracy

There are at least two distinct criticisms of attempts to link green thinking with deliberative democratic theory. The first is a general antipathy towards accounts of political agency: it is argued that a green theory of value must take precedence over any particular form of political institution. What is the guarantee that deliberative institutions will embody environmental values? The second area of dispute arises with respect to the human-centredness of communicative practices. At their strongest, such criticisms hold that deliberative politics is illegitimate in limiting the participants in any discourse to human actors only; at their weakest, it is argued that certain types of epistemological and ethical claims central to particular environmental values cannot be appealed to in deliberative institutions. We shall attend to these two areas of conflict in turn.

In his book *Green Political Theory*, Goodin argues: 'To advocate democracy is to advocate procedures, to advocate environmentalism is to advocate substantive outcomes: what guarantee can we have that the former procedures will yield the latter sorts of outcomes?' (Goodin, 1992: 168). Similarly, Andrew Dobson notes that 'there is no guarantee that the free and equal conversations will grant a more valued status to the non-human natural world than it has at present' (Dobson, 1993: 198). Both writers are correct in declaring that deliberative politics cannot *guarantee* that environmental values will necessarily be given a higher priority in decisions. All that can be guaranteed is that the values we associate with the non-human world can at least be articulated and defended. All voices have the right to be heard – those who wish to emphasise environmental values should not be restricted. However, an equal right to be heard does not guarantee priority in judgements and decisions. Greens (and others) must provide convincing reasons as to why particular environmental values should be given priority.

Goodin's argument about the significance of democracy in green political thought rests on his claim that a 'green theory of agency cannot be *derived from* the green theory of value' (Goodin, 1992: 168). The main focus of green politics should be the promotion of core green values and the protection of the environment: a commitment to a particular form of democracy cannot be derived from these core values and is therefore a secondary consideration. At one level, he is right: political and social arrangements cannot be 'read off' from the values we associate with the non-human world (Saward, 1993: 69). However, Goodin believes that there is actually a single source of value at the heart of green thinking that should predominate over all other considerations: 'naturalness'. The products of natural processes, untouched by human hands, provides the larger context and continuity within which we understand our life plans and projects (Goodin, 1992: 30–40). Greens should concern themselves with achieving outcomes that embody this green theory of value; procedures for achieving this are secondary.

The emphasis within green ethical and political theory on a guarantee of green outcomes is characteristic of a 'latent authoritarian tendency, an impulse to secure a principle by putting it beyond dispute' (Torgerson, 1999: 126; also Saward, 1993; Taylor, 1996). Ecocentric theorists who express green principles as non-negotiable imperatives threaten to overwhelm and silence all other considerations, including a commitment to democracy. As Douglas Torgerson argues: 'The ecocentric position in environmental ethics ... presses toward a definitive conclusion: a philosophical reconceptualisation of the human/nature relationship that can provide a final moral standard not to be questioned, but obeyed' (Torgerson, 1999: 105). The contingency and uncertainty inherent in decision making within democratic institutions becomes unacceptable to more fundamentalist greens.

Not only should we be concerned with the potentially authoritarian impulse within green political theory, but we need also to recognise that Goodin's account of value is itself contested. As we argued in Chapter 1, there is a *plurality of values* that we associate with the non-human world. If (contrary to Goodin) there is no single decision rule to order these and other values, then we require political processes that allow for reasoned dialogue, the disclosure of different value orientations and opportunities for challenge, reflection and judgement. But environmental ethics has little or nothing to say about how to mediate different moral claims (Taylor, 1996: 95). As we discussed earlier in this chapter, Goodin has more recently accepted that greens should give their qualified support to deliberative democracy over other forms of political arrangement on the basis that citizens are more likely to internalise the interests of the non-human world (Goodin, 1996). The success of such internalisation requires civic responsiveness on the part of participants who do not share an ecocentric sensibility and civic endurance on the part of more radical greens in their attempt to persuade these sceptics. There is no guarantee that all decisions will embody environmental values, but, as Tim Hayward wryly observes: 'If ecocentrism is "true", then this is a truth, like any other, which will be proved in practice' (T. Hayward, 1995: 98).

Dobson's recognition that deliberative practices would not necessarily 'grant a more valued status to the non-human natural world than it has at present' (Dobson, 1993: 198) is both a general point and one made with specific reference to Habermas. Habermas has become a particular target for green political thought because of the ethical and epistemological limits he places on what can be the basis of a justified claim in deliberation. Criticisms of Habermas's strict separation of discourses of moral, ethical and pragmatic concerns (and his earlier work on quasi-transcendental cognitive interests) are compelling but do not undermine the broader conception of deliberative politics offered here. Many of the green criticisms are actually arguments against his conception of *discourse ethics* rather than deliberative democracy.[16] However, it is worth briefly engaging with these arguments as much of the green antipathy toward deliberative politics lies here.

The ecocentric critique of Habermas rests on the inability of discourse ethics to grant nature moral status: within this conceptual framework, nature cannot be conceived as an end-in-itself. In the hands of Habermas, discourse ethics (and the earlier theory of human interests) precludes an appeal to the intrinsic value of non-human nature (Whitebook, 1979; Ottmann, 1982; Eckersley, 1992; 1999). Although Habermas has rarely discussed environmental issues (Habermas, 1982: 238–50; 1993: 105–11),[17] he displays a level of ecological sensibility in his awareness of 'the destabilising intervention into ecological systems and natural milieux, the destruction of traditional forms of life, the threat to the communicative internal structures of the life-worlds, the depletion of non-regenerable natural and cultural resources, the negative side effects of capitalist growth, monetarisation, legislation, bureaucratization, and so on' (Habermas, 1982: 241). In a later piece he recognises that:

> aside from prudential considerations, there are good *ethical reasons* that speak in favour of the protection of plants and species, reasons that become apparent once we ask ourselves seriously how, as members of a civilised global society, we want to live on this planet and how, as members of our own species, we want to treat other species. In certain respects, *aesthetic reasons* have here even greater force than the ethical, for in the aesthetic experience of nature, things withdraw into an unapproachable autonomy and inaccessibility; they then exhibit their fragile integrity so clearly that they strike us as inviolable in their own right and not merely as desirable elements of a preferred form of life.
>
> (Habermas, 1993: 111)

His account of the value of non-human nature bears more than a passing resemblance to the earlier characterisation of environmentally sensitive value pluralism in Chapter 1.

Habermas recognises many of the values that we have argued are associated with the non-human world. However, his criticism of environmental ethics and politics is twofold: first, that intrinsic value theory is ethically and epistemologically nonsensical; and, second, that it makes no sense to talk of human–non-human relations in terms of what he delineates as 'morality'. Critics such as Eckersley, are, then, right to argue that, according to Habermas's schema, non-human entities cannot be *morally* considerable subjects (Eckersley,

1992: 111). This simply follows from his delineation of 'the moral' wherein 'the in principle egalitarian relation of reciprocity built into communicative action . . . cannot be carried over into the relations between humans and nature in any strict sense' (Habermas, 1982: 248). Habermas has gone some way in recognising that we may well have a quasi-communicative responsibility towards some animals, based on the deep-seated vulnerability that they share with human subjects (Habermas, 1993: 109), although critics contend that these comments are highly underdeveloped and contrived (Vogel, 1996; Eckersley, 1999: 36).

But Eckersley does not wish to give up on 'greening' discourse ethics. She argues that discourse ethics can be extended to give moral consideration to non-human nature: 'it is not necessary that a being be a *morally responsible agent* in order to receive recognition as a *morally considerable subject or being* . . . it is enough that a being is a centre of agency, however rudimentary, with its own life and special mode of flourishing for it to be recognised as a morally considerable being, deserving recognition and consideration in human deliberation' (Eckersley, 1999: 42).[18] The inability to reciprocate moral recognition should not disqualify non-human entities from moral consideration. Drawing on Hannah Arendt's conception of 'representative thinking' (another way of expressing 'enlarged mentality'), Eckersley argues that non-human entities can be included as 'imaginary partners in conversation', with participants 'anticipating and assuming the position of others in order to test and evaluate the consequences of proposed norms from all conceivable perspectives', including the perspectives of non-human entities (ibid.: 27). Just as in actual deliberations, when not all humans will be present and their perspectives will have to be represented, Eckersley believes that the perspectives of non-human nature can also be represented.

Eckersley's revision of discourse ethics remains controversial, and our brief analysis of intrinsic value theories offered in Chapter 1 is critical of such positions. Quite simply, Habermas and Eckersley have different conceptions of what constitutes 'the moral', and of whether nature can be the subject of moral theory. However, in the realm of deliberative democratic *politics* (rather than discourse *ethics*), ecocentric theorists such as Eckersley are free to offer arguments about extending moral consideration to non-human nature and promoting representative thinking beyond species boundaries. Aside from claims that would undermine the context of deliberation itself, we cannot pre-judge what is and what is not a permissible claim in democratic dialogue; that is for those involved in the dialogue to judge.[19] Ecocentrics committed to the intrinsic value of nature are not precluded from disclosing their arguments in deliberations and attempting to persuade other citizens of their cogency. However, a number of important questions which are pertinent to democratic practice remain outstanding from Eckersley's reconstruction of discourse ethics. As Eckersley herself is well aware, her position leaves unanswered the question of who is to speak for nature, and on what grounds? Who has the necessary knowledge or expertise (Eckersley, 1999: 33–4)? We will return to the special problem of ecological advocacy and representation in the final chapter, but we need to remind ourselves again of the danger that claims to moral status may rest on the 'privileged' access of the ecocentric theorist and may be seen as a definitive conclusion beyond democratic struggle: the fundamentalist impulse within ecocentrism must be avoided, otherwise it undermines the very conditions of deliberation.

In some respects, Dryzek has taken the discussion of the status of nature in deliberative processes further than Eckersley by arguing that our limited understanding of communication privileges the human species. Dryzek is seeking 'more egalitarian interchange at the human/ natural boundary ... more effective integration of political and ecological communication' (Dryzek, 2000a: 146). Our understanding of communication can be extended to include non-human entities by affording a recognition of agency in nature.[20]

> The key would be to treat communication, and so communicative rationality, as extending to entities that can act as agents, even though they lack the self-awareness that connotes subjectivity. Agency is not the same as subjectivity, and only the former need be sought in nature. Habermas treats nature as though it were brute matter. But nature is not passive, inert, and plastic. Instead, this world is truly alive, and pervaded with meanings.
>
> (Dryzek, 2000a: 148)

Is Dryzek's further assertion of agency in nature helpful? How far does the recognition of agency take us? It is true that the natural world is 'alive' and that it is 'pervaded with meanings'. But these are meanings *for* humanity. It is humans that value, it is humans that discover meaning. And how helpful is it to think of agency in nature? Is this simply a metaphorical image or a literal belief in nature as a democratic subject (Torgerson, 1999: 125; also Vogel, 1996)? The ascription of agency usually implies a sense of reflexivity, an ability to reflect on moral obligations. On closer examination, Dryzek's use of the term 'agency' and his desire to ascribe it to the natural world appears little more than a repetition of his call for political institutions to be more sensitive toward negative feedback signals. There is no need to reconceptualise deliberative democracy – the conditions that underpin deliberation already allow us to 'treat signals emanating from the natural world with the same respect we accord signals emanating from human subjects, and as requiring equally careful interpretation' (Dryzek, 1995: 21). Without reconceptualising nature as an 'agent' or a 'communicative partner', we can still agree with Dryzek that for 'green democrats, the regulative ideal is effectiveness in communication that transcends the boundary of the human world' (Dryzek, 2000a: 145).

The promise of deliberative democracy for greens is that the plurality of environmental values will be voiced and considered in the political process. This is not an argument that there is a necessary connection between environmental values and deliberative democracy. Neither is there any *guarantee* that decisions emerging from deliberative processes will necessarily embody environmental values. However, it is worth reflecting that, as currently practised, there is a guarantee that in decision-making procedures such as CBA environmental values *cannot* be adequately represented. Deliberative democracy at the very least opens up the political space for the plurality of values to be articulated and to be considered in the policy process.

From critique to institutional design

This chapter has focused heavily on the potential merits of deliberative democratic theory. But it has, for the most part, remained a highly abstract and theoretical discussion. Deliberative democracy offers a powerful theoretical position for the political critique of actually existing institutions in terms of their failure to ensure both inclusiveness and unconstrained dialogue. However, if deliberative democracy is to be understood as a constructive project, then it needs to engage with the detailed and messy task of how democratic deliberation might be institutionalised. This need is generally recognised by theorists, although comparatively little work has been done on institutional design. If such work remains purely aspirational, we are left in the rather uncomfortable and unsustainable position of contrasting actual practices of liberal democracy (e.g. the use of CBA) with an ideal theoretical construction (deliberative democracy).

But when we turn to the constructive project of institutional design, it becomes clear that deliberative democracy is far from being a *complete* theory of democracy. At the beginning of this chapter, a broad characterisation of deliberative democracy was offered: democratic legitimacy rests on inclusiveness and unconstrained dialogue orientated toward mutual understanding. Such characteristics underdetermine institutional design. As Judith Squires neatly states: 'No comprehensive theory of democracy can focus on deliberation alone' (Squires, 2002: 133). Deliberative democracy lacks a theory of collective choice or a decision rule (Manin, 1997: 189; Saward, 1998a: 64). At some point, decisions need to be made and preferences aggregated in some manner; and yet there is no decision-making principle implicit within deliberative democratic theory. Deliberative democracy should not be understood as a self-contained 'model of democracy', but rather as a 'desirable ingredient' of democracy (Saward, 2000a: 68). This does not necessarily undermine its theoretical promise, but it does mean that we need to understand how democratic deliberation might be 'blended' with other institutional goods and structures.

Deliberative democracy emerged in response to the perceived failings of liberal democratic theory and practice, and much writing critiques contemporary institutions: the deliberative model is typically positively contrasted with a (liberal) aggregative model of democracy.[21] But we need to be clear that deliberative theories cannot be contrasted with aggregation per se. Politics needs decisions: the 'economy of time' haunts political institutions (Beetham, 1992). In some ways, the very idea of a deliberative decision-making institution exhibits a certain paradoxical quality – tensions may exist between the need for a decision and the institutionalisation of deliberation (Mansbridge, 1996: 47). A decision implies the *end* of a discursive process. But deliberation is, in principle, ongoing: excepting universal consensus, there is no obvious end-point to the process of mutual understanding, reasoned dialogue, persuasion and judgement. On the other hand, politics requires decisions: there is a temporal limitation to debate. Here, we witness tensions between the goods of mutual understanding and efficiency (Chambers, 1995: 241). Deliberative democratic theory says little about actual decision rules, only that collective decisions should be informed by reflective preferences. After a process of deliberation, the nature of aggregation procedures, such as the majoritarian principle, is altered. Although the decision does not affirm all points of view, all perspectives have been taken into consideration. As Manin argues: 'the procedure preceding the decision is a condition for legitimacy, which is just as necessary as the majority principle. It is the conjunction of these elements that creates legitimacy' (Manin, 1987: 359).

Given the lack of attention to the design of decision-making institutions, we find that many theories of deliberative democracy are actually assimilated with the institutions of liberal constitutionalism (Dryzek, 2000b). As Squires contends, 'the current institutions of representative democracy are explicitly critiqued within the deliberative democracy literature, they are also . . . implicitly assumed' (Squires, 2002: 134). Habermas, for example, recognises the importance of a liberal constitution in protecting and nurturing will-formation within the public sphere. The informal deliberations of the public sphere are to influence the more formal deliberations and decision making of the institutions of government (Habermas, 1996b).

Disappointed by the assimilation of deliberative democracy to liberal constitutionalism, and concerned that deliberative institutions will be coopted and absorbed by the state, Dryzek has developed a theory of *discursive* democracy. His is an alternative to the current dominant trajectory of deliberative democracy and attempts to retain the critical orientation toward the institutions of the liberal state. His theory of discursive democracy avoids the question of decision rules in political institutions and instead privileges the deliberations and discourses within civil society, celebrating in particular the activities of new social movements (Dryzek, 2000a,b). He is highly sceptical of the possibility of authentic deliberation within state structures (although in rare circumstances it may be possible). As he argues: 'the key difference is that discursive democracy problematises the democratic potential of the state in the way liberal constitutionalism does not' (Dryzek, 2000b: 82).

However, even Dryzek recognises that the connection between the public sphere and forms of political authority must be attended to:

> The authenticity of *democracy* requires ... that ... reflective preferences influence collective outcomes, and so both an orientation to the state and discursive mechanisms for the transmission of public opinion to the state are required, so long as the state is the main (though far from exclusive) locus of collective decision.
>
> (Dryzek, 2000a: 162)

There is a recognition on the part of deliberative democrats (of different hues) that the 'mechanisms for the transmission of public opinion to the state' are of particular interest if the reflective judgements of citizens are to affect political decision-making processes. And this is where deliberative democracy is confronted with offering alternative designs to sophisticated procedures utilised by liberal democratic states, including CBA.

We will have reason to return to competing conceptions of deliberative democracy and the different locations of dialogue in the final chapter. However, the task of the next chapter is to judge whether alternative institutions can be designed that might improve on the practice of CBA in responding to the plurality of environmental values. In particular, can institutions be designed that ensure inclusiveness and unconstrained dialogue and provide for reflection on environmental values? In this sense, the institutional designs discussed are offered as potential supplements or reforms to the existing liberal democratic political architecture. Drawing lessons from this analysis, we will move on in the final chapter to speculate on more radical institutional changes that might form part of a politics of ecological democratisation.

As we make this decisive move from political critique to constructive institutional design, the voices of sceptics will loom larger still. In the move from the theoretical realm to practical design we will do well to consider Eckersley's warning that 'it is foolhardy to make "heroic assumptions" about the motivations of political actors in democratic deliberation, especially when considering institutional re-design' (Eckersley, 2000: 124; also Johnson, 1998: 173–4). Are we expecting too much from citizens in expecting them to display the moral courage necessary in cultivating an enlarged mentality and acknowledging conflicting values? Mutual understanding is a fragile good: 'misunderstanding, rejection, withdrawal and conflict' are also possible (Young, 1990a: 310). Citizens will require 'a confidence that the generative aspects of democracy are sufficient to allay or contain the anxieties and fears of politics' (Warren, 1996b: 251). Can institutions be designed that enhance and protect democratic deliberation? Factors that might undermine dialogue, including the insidious exercise of power, inequalities of resources, the economy of time, and limited knowledge and experience, must be recognised and accounted for in thinking through the potential shape of deliberative institutions that are sensitive to the plurality of environmental values.

Conclusion

There is no necessary connection between environmental values and deliberative democracy: deliberation cannot guarantee that decisions will always meet with the approval of greens. However, the cultivation of democratic deliberation offers a conducive context within which the plurality of environmental values and perspectives on the non-human world can be voiced and considered in the political process. It provides conditions under which the conflict between environmental (and other) values can be appreciated, and solutions to complex environmental problems sought. There are good reasons for greens to support the embedding of democratic deliberation in contemporary political institutions. Just how such embedding or institutionalisation of deliberation might take place is the central concern of the remaining two chapters of this book. We begin with an assessment of three different 'deliberative models' through which the reflective opinions of citizens might be transmitted to decision makers.

4 Three deliberative models

The theoretical promise of enhancing democratic deliberation within the decision-making process is attractive to greens. The institutionalisation of deliberation offers a context within which the plurality of environmental values can be effectively articulated and considered. For the most part, the work on the relationship between deliberative democracy and environmental politics remains a theoretical discussion, with little or no detailed debate on questions of institutional design. The pressure, then, is on advocates to move beyond the simply aspirational. Greens may have good reason to express interest in democratic deliberation, but, if the constructive and practical element of institutional design is not developed, that interest will wane.

This chapter begins the constructive and practical task of thinking through the institutional implications of deliberative democracy. It begins with a brief overview of debates about institutional structure within the theoretical literatures on green politics and deliberative democracy. The main body of the chapter investigates three potential 'deliberative models' that could promote increased participation and deliberation by citizens in the decision-making process: mediation, citizen forums, and referendums and citizen initiatives. Our interest is in the extent to which these institutions enhance democratic dialogue and consideration of environmental values.

Trends in institutional design

When it comes to institutional design, radical decentralisation has become a touchstone for green politics. One thing that deep and social ecologists can agree on is that small-scale, autonomous and self-sufficient political units are preferred, typically defined by ecological (or bioregional) boundaries. There are a number of good reasons why deliberative democrats might also support such local political control. For example, regular face-to-face participation in decision making is made possible, and increased knowledge and sensitivity to ecological conditions is likely if the political community is dependent on local environmental resources. However, a number of problems arise with such a blanket commitment to local autonomy and face-to-face participation. Two will concern us here. First, there has been a lack of detailed work on institutional design within green politics. It is simply assumed that face-to-face participation is more democratic. However, studies of face-to-face assemblies have shown that they are not necessarily democratic panaceas and are easily manipulated by powerful and experienced citizens (Mansbridge, 1983: 276–7; Sanders, 1997). Democratic deliberation will not necessarily emerge 'naturally' in face-to-face environments. The detailed structure of institutions needs to be attended to. Second, the local level is not always the most suitable for dealing with the scale and complexity of many environmental problems, which may require higher levels of political coordination. The question of institutional design that enables engagement across political communities is poorly developed. Deliberative democracy is not necessarily contiguous with direct, face-to-face visions of democracy.

A more ecologically sensitive approach is that based on the idea of 'appropriate scale'. Here the principles of democratic deliberation point to all affected interests having a voice. The relevant political community for ecological problems cannot be fixed and needs to be sensitive to the scope and scale of the particular issue (Benhabib, 1996: 70; Christoff, 1996b). Robyn Eckersley, for example, has argued for the development of a 'democracy of the affected' (Eckersley, 2000). However, as Michael Saward recognises, institutionalising the 'all affected principle' raises a number of practical questions about 'who can be said to be affected (moderately? significantly?)' and the apparent requirement for 'a different constituency – in effect, a new political unit – each time a collective decision needs to be made' (Saward, 1998a: 125).[1]

If greens are looking to deliberative democrats to give them guidance on questions of institutional structure then generally they will be disappointed. It is a fair criticism of the deliberative democracy literature that it generally remains a highly abstract and theoretical endeavour – that it fails to systematically engage in the 'messy' and more detailed task of institutional design. In particular, there has been a lack of detailed analysis of institutions that would allow for the political engagement of citizens in the decision-making process. Much of the work on institutions concentrates on one of three areas. First, theorists concern themselves with the 'constitution' of deliberative democracy – the rights and principles that are the necessary conditions for the emergence and sustenance of democratic dialogue and judgement (Cohen, 1989; Benhabib, 1992; Gutmann and Thompson, 1996; Habermas, 1996b). Second, there is a burgeoning literature on the reform of legislatures, particularly focusing on assuring presence for marginalised groups such as women and ethnic minorities (Young, 1990b; Phillips, 1995; Squires, 1999). Both Eckersley and Andrew Dobson have offered arguments for the proxy-representation of non-citizens (in particular future generations and non-human nature) (Dobson, 1996b; Eckersley, 2000). We shall have reason to return to the question of representation later, when tensions between deliberation and representation will be discussed. Third, beyond the discussion of constitutional rights and principles and representation, a significant number of theorists focus particular attention on associations of civil society, such as interest groups, political parties and social movements, as the institutions that promote democratic deliberation (Cohen, 1989, 1996; Benhabib, 1996; Mansbridge, 1996; Dryzek, 2000a,b). That an active civil society and reinvigorated public sphere are necessary components of deliberative politics is unquestionable, especially with respect to the development of democratic citizenship.' However, there is generally little sense of how the deliberations from within civil society are to be transmitted to the more formal arena of political decision making.

There is, then, a sharp distinction within the deliberative democracy literature between a focus on constitutions/legislatures and on the associations of civil society.[2] Given that our interest in this chapter is the 'discursive mechanisms for the transmission of public opinion to the state' (Dryzek, 2000a: 162), this is somewhat disappointing. As

James Bohman argues in a survey article on deliberative democracy, 'there is still a surprising lack of empirical case studies of democratic deliberation at the appropriate level and scale' (Bohman, 1998: 419). John Dryzek is one of the few theorists whose work has been particularly sensitive to questions of institutional structure. In *Discursive Democracy*, he displays some dissatisfaction with critical theorists who refuse to engage in institutional design, and briefly discusses a small number of incipient discursive designs which are 'located in, and help constitute, a public space within which citizens associate and confront the state' (Dryzek, 1990b: 43), namely mediation and regulatory negotiation (ibid.: 45–8). We shall have reason to return to these designs below, but, like the critical theorists before him, Dryzek remains deeply concerned about the cooption and absorption of discursive designs by state and corporate actors (ibid.: 81), and in the end much of his work mirrors that of other critical theorists in its celebration of the public sphere of civil society and, in particular, the activities of new social movements (Dryzek, 2000a,b).

Given the paucity of work available, the rest of this chapter engages with the possible deliberative design of such 'mechanisms of transmission of public opinion'. Three 'models' are offered: mediation; citizen forums; and citizen initiatives and referendums. The models are far from exhaustive, but have distinctive characteristics and differences that are worth reflecting on. Mediation relies on the participation of 'stakeholders', where the representatives of affected interests are directly involved in conflict resolution or problem solving. Citizen forums allow a random sample of citizens to come together to discuss issues of public concern. Initiatives and referendums provide for direct voting on constitutional, legislative or policy issues by the whole population. All three models have been used to varying extents in the development of environmental policy.

In analysing the three models, we need to bear in mind a number of relevant characteristics that can be drawn from our preceding discussions of deliberative and green theory. In all cases we will wish to assess the extent to which institutions achieve:

1   *Inclusiveness*: are all voices heard? If not, how are they represented?
2   *Unconstrained dialogue*: is deliberation defended against strategic action on the part of powerful interests? Are the conditions in

place for the cultivation of judgement as enlarged mentality?

3 *A just decision*: what type of decision rule is in operation? Does this affect the nature of deliberations?

4 *Sensitivity to environmental values and conditions*: can the plurality of environmental values be articulated? Are deliberations and decisions sensitive to the scope, scale and complexity of environmental issues?[3]

The three models are offered primarily to stimulate debate about the detail of institutional design within green politics – calling for more participation or deliberation is not enough. The task must be to answer the questions 'What sort of participation?' and 'Deliberation under what conditions?'. Initially, the models are offered as potential complements to existing decision-making processes, but in the next chapter we will discuss the extent to which they might form part of a more radical project of ecological democratisation. Therefore, these designs ought to be of interest whether the focus is on 'collective ecological management', in which deliberative institutions would complement the representative structures of the green state (Barry, 1999), or on a more radical 'commons' or 'bioregional' approach, in which the role of the state is minimised or even removed and local communities take control of their local bioregions (*The Ecologist*, 1993). In both cases, detailed work on the form of institutions is needed.

Model 1: mediation and stakeholder group engagement

Mediation brings together different parties who are in dispute and aims to achieve resolution of conflict such that all parties involved are satisfied and in agreement as to the way forward. Proponents of mediation argue that its value rests on it being a voluntary, non-adversarial and cooperative process in which parties focus on collective concerns rather than purely private interests. Mediators play a fundamental role in the generation of the conditions required for a successful dispute resolution process, although they have no authority to impose a settlement. As such, mediation inhabits the space between unassisted negotiation and binding arbitration (Susskind and Cruikshank, 1987). Reflection on the practice of assisted negotiations may shed some light on potential problems or opportunities of *unassisted* forms of negotiation and problem solving often promoted by greens, such as round tables and associative democracy.

Most commonly associated with labour relations, mediation has been a developing area of practice in responding to environmental disputes and conflicts, particularly in the United States, since the 1970s. Initially, environmental mediation tended to focus on sporadic local, site-specific disputes. However, it has expanded into areas of policy dialogue and regulatory negotiation, and in certain domains has become formalised and institutionalised; for example, at least two federal directives promote mediation over litigation (Blackburn and Bruce, 1995: 2). An extensive literature by practitioners and theorists has emerged, although it is surprising that few connections have been made with deliberative democracy.

There appear to be good reasons why deliberative theorists should be interested in mediation: a variety of affected interests are present and thus there is potential for 'collaborative inquiry' (Susskind and Cruikshank, 1987: 29–30), the development of mutual understanding and trust (Baughman, 1995: 263; Hadden, 1995: 244), and the stimulation of social learning and re-evaluation of interests (Amy, 1987: 61). Any negotiated settlement or decision is more likely to be implemented, simply because it has been assented to voluntarily by all parties to the dispute. The stakeholders 'own' the decision – it is not imposed by an outside body.

However, critics of mediation point to a number of features of the process that undermine its democratic potential, instead reinforcing both existing power differentials and the systematic advantage of dominant political and economic interests in society. First, there is the question of representation and presence. Typically, environmentalists will be at an organisational and financial disadvantage in comparison with other corporate interests (such as businesses and government agencies) (Fiorino, 1995; Hadden, 1995). Second, inequalities of representation and voice are further compounded by the underlying understanding of the nature of conflicts within much mediation theory and practice. Critics argue that mediation involves a high degree of agenda setting in that it encourages us to see environmental problems as unique, isolated phenomena abstracted from social relations, because these kind of problems are easiest to mediate. Third, it is argued that the theory of dispute resolution treats the interests of parties as given and incorrigible (Ellison, 1991: 248). The neutrality of the mediator, seeking a compromise between static clashes of interests, is seen as a virtue to be cultivated. The ethical, public-regarding arguments of greens are compromised because they have no more standing than purely self-interested preferences (Amy, 1987: 185; Forester, 1992: 261; Dukes, 1996: 115–6). Fourth, the informality of mediation – one of the features of the process that is celebrated for encouraging parties to explore new territory – may actually invite abuse. Mediation can 'disarm participants of their legitimate feelings of outrage and frustration' (Amy, 1987: 126), pressurising them 'toward forms of reasonableness' and illegitimate consensus (Ellison, 1991: 255).

For those advocates of mediation who remain convinced of its democratic potential, these are serious charges. One line of response is to ask whether critics expect too much from mediation – after all, traditional liberal democratic processes are equally criticised for their failure to challenge dominant power relations (Dryzek, 1987; Forester, 1992: 270; Dukes, 1996: 20).

But, on a more constructive note, the deliberative democratic potential of mediation is clearly tied to the role played by the *mediator*. Many of the criticisms focus on the idea of the mediator as a neutral 'referee', overseeing a contest of interests – a passive form of neutrality simply ensures the perpetuation of the status quo, reinforces existing inequalities of power and legitimises disparities. The deliberative democratic potential of mediation rests on mediators taking an *activist* stance toward the mediation process (Susskind and Ozawa, 1985; Forester, 1992; Dukes, 1996). It requires a recognition that the process and substance of policy debate will itself shape and influence preferences and that mediators 'must nurture a process of public deliberation and learning, a process of civic discovery' (Forester, 1992: 260). John Forester argues that mediators assume a 'public-creating responsibility':

> Once the environmental mediator... makes judgements about and manages 'appropriate participation', that mediator-facilitator has assumed a public-creating responsibility – indeed a constituting or constitutional responsibility – to structure public interaction, debate, and the process of dispute management or settlement ... For mediator-facilitators in practice create political spaces in which conflicting parties speak and listen, recollect their experiences and express their needs, articulate their interests

and invoke their commitments . . . Fulfilling this public-creating responsibility requires mediator-facilitators to *protect and nurture* an always precarious and contingent democratic public sphere.

(Forester, 1992: 263–4)

It is important to recognise that impartiality is not abandoned; rather, mediators play a fundamental role in creating the conditions for public deliberation and ensuring that all parties are present and able to articulate their perspectives, access information and challenge and question other parties. The mediator usually establishes initial lines of communication between parties, disseminates information and helps set the rules for engagement. Mediators will play a role in ensuring that affected interests are suitably represented and that there are mechanisms through which representatives are able to engage with their constituencies (Susskind and Ozawa, 1985). An active mediator advocates and defends a particular type of process, 'seeking certain qualities of outcome, including fairness, inclusiveness, openness and endurance' (Dukes, 1996: 176). Such an interpretation of the mediation process offers a more favourable climate for the normative concerns of greens.

This still leaves the question of cooption. Lawrence Susskind and Connie Ozawa are fairly blunt when they suggest that if representatives are unhappy then they should walk away from the process (Susskind and Ozawa, 1985: 146). Further, participants will often be required to seek authorisation from their constituency. As Douglas Amy argues, this is the 'last line of defence' against the seduction of mediation: 'the constituents act as the ultimate safeguard against selling-out' (Amy, 1987: 118). If the representatives are unable to explain the negotiated settlement to their constituents then perhaps this can be traced to the cooption of the representative by other parties.

Mediation takes a number of forms in practice – some examples will confirm all the worst criticisms of the sceptics; others will offer grounds for the belief that a meaningful public forum has been created. The possibility of engendering democratic deliberation and civic discovery certainly warrants close attention to the structure and context of the mediation process. And, in terms of scope and scale, mediation offers a model that translates from local to international-level disputes. Although there is little practice of mediation in the environmental field at the international level, Dryzek argues that there is great potential for dispute resolution and problem-solving processes. In particular, there are accepted and recognised global problems, and 'willing, competent, and credible' intermediaries such as the United Nations, third-party governments and academic institutions. However, the unequal capabilities of different states, and their potential unwillingness to deal with non-state actors, raises concerns (Dryzek, 1990b: 90ff.).

Lessons may be learnt from the practice of mediation for other 'stakeholder' approaches. A growing number of international environmental bodies and regimes have begun to provide non-governmental organisations (NGOs) with increasing access. The United Nations Commission on Sustainable Development (UNCSD), created in 1993 to review progress on Agenda 21, is one interesting example. Not only are reports received from national governments, but representations are also made by accredited NGOs.[4] The effectiveness of UNCSD can be questioned, but it is an example of the emergence of more innovative institutional design in response to growing pressures to include non-state actors in international regimes (Connelly and Smith, 2003: 245–6). At the national and local level, the Agenda 21 process has been central to the development of national round tables, such as the UK Sustainable Development Commission (UKSDC) and Local Agenda 21 forums, in which non-governmental organisations typically play key roles.[5] The UKSDC has a membership drawn from all sectors (including environmental NGOs), and part of its role is to build consensus on the actions needed if further progress towards sustainable development is to be achieved (ibid.: 315–6).

There are two obvious major differences between mediation and stakeholder approaches. First, mediation tends to be a one-off conflict resolution or problem-solving process; the latter institutional arrangements are long term. Second, mediation processes have the most deliberative potential when the mediator plays an activist 'public-creating' role. There is no direct equivalent to such mediators in other stakeholder designs. The tendency is towards forms of state-sponsored corporatism. Dryzek argues that there is evidence that corporatist arrangements have proved more effective in achieving positive environmental policy outcomes and that it is 'the state model most conducive to a discursive and democratic civil society' (Dryzek, 2000a: 107). The question, then, rests on whether an activist green state is a real possibility (Barry, 1999) or whether corporatism is nothing more than an elaborate form of the cooption and absorption of groups by the state.

Where the stakeholder models are perhaps at their weakest is in terms of direct citizen participation. In all cases, it is representatives of various constituencies who are directly involved in decision making: deliberation is mediated by representation. Often, it will be established environmental pressure groups that engage in stakeholder forums. For some this is not a problem: given the complexity of contemporary societies, citizens do not have the time, desire or expertise to engage continually in the critical scrutiny of political and scientific authority: 'One important function of public pressure groups in a democratic setting is that they constitute a critical and attentive public' (Warren, 1996b: 56). This may be the case, but there remains the question of authorisation of representatives and associations (Susskind and Ozawa, 1985) and the related issue of institutionalising deliberation not only between, but also within, associations. As Jane Mansbridge rightly suggests, deliberation needs to be institutionalised not only between elites, but also between elites and rank and file, and among the rank and file within associations, otherwise 'a narrowly self-interested citizenry will eventually throw out its public-spirited representatives' (Mansbridge, 1995: 143–4). Few environmental (or other) associations or pressure groups even begin to approach such an internal institutionalisation of deliberation, and tensions may well exist between the idea of group representation and the requirement within deliberative democracy for representatives to be open to the possibility of transformation (Rosenblum, 1998: 343–6). This tension will be discussed further in the next chapter.

Model 2: citizen forums

In recent years, there has been growing interest in innovative democratic experiments, such as deliberative opinion polls, citizens' juries and consensus conferences, which provide the space for citizens to deliberate on pressing policy issues. These three types of 'citizen forums'[6] share a number of features: a cross-section of the population is brought together for three to four days to discuss an issue of public concern; citizens are exposed to a variety of information and hear a wide range of views from witnesses whom they are able to cross-examine; and the fairness of the proceedings is entrusted to an independent facilitating organisation.

There are, however, some important differences between the three designs. First, there are variations in the number of citizens who participate. Deliberative opinion polls have involved between 200 and 466 citizens. In comparison, a citizens' jury or consensus conference will typically only involve between twelve and twenty-five citizens.[7] Second, to select citizens, deliberative opinion polls and citizens' juries use some form of random sampling procedure. Because of the relatively small size of most citizens' juries, citizens are often selected using stratified random sampling to ensure that different demographic, and at times attitudinal, criteria are fulfilled. The sheer size of a deliberative opinion poll means that stratification is unnecessary. Consensus conferences differ again in that volunteers are recruited through advertisements and make written applications from which the panel is selected on the basis of socio-demographic criteria. Thus, the first stage of the procedure is self-selecting. However, there is an element of self-selection in both citizens' juries and deliberative opinion polling, given that citizens who are randomly selected still have the choice of whether to accept the invitation to attend. The final important distinction rests with the outcome of the different models. With juries and consensus conferences, citizens come to *collective* decisions after a period of deliberation and provide a series of recommendations as a group. By comparison, at the end of the deliberative opinion poll, the *individual* views of citizens are recorded. As the name suggests, there is a post-deliberation opinion poll.

Deliberative democrats have shown significant interest in the potential of citizen forums (Fishkin, 1997; Fishkin and Luskin, 2000; Smith, 2000; Smith and Wales, 2000). Although such forums can only approximate the ideal of inclusiveness and equality of voice through sampling procedures, they do foster conditions under which informed and democratic deliberation can take place and directly involve citizens from a cross-section of society. Suspicion of strategic action on the part of citizens is lessened, given that these forums do not 'represent an opportunity for advancement, promotion or election' for those involved (Dienel, 1996: 114). Important evidence is emerging from these experiments that indicates that citizens take their role seriously and are willing and able to reflect on different evidence and experiences.

In a number of citizens' juries, for example, citizens have spent time developing ground rules to ensure fair and equal deliberations (Smith and Wales, 1999: 303). Citizens become better informed, and many of their preferences and judgements change. There is also some indication that citizens are more civically minded and active long after the processes have ended (Mayer *et al.*, 1995; Fishkin, 1997; Smith and Wales, 1999). Empirical backing is beginning to emerge for the theoretical claim made for the transformative and educative power of democratic deliberation. As with mediation, facilitators in citizen forums play an important role in ensuring inclusiveness, encouraging an ethos of mutual respect and defending against domination and manipulation by witnesses or participants during deliberations.

Citizen forums have been run in a variety of contexts, on a wide variety of issues and with different levels of impact on political authorities. All three models have been used at some point on broadly environmental issues. Under the guidance of its originator, James Fishkin, about twenty deliberative opinion polls have been run in the United States, UK and Australia, tackling a range of public issues. Many of these have received a high level of media exposure and public interest. Roughly half of the polls have been run by public utilities in the state of Texas, to fulfil their requirement for public participation in resource planning (Fishkin, 1997: 200–3; Center for Deliberative Polling, 2001). The results from the first three utility polls offer interesting reading. Presented with four 'first choice' options (renewable energy; fossil fuel plants; investment in energy conservation; or buying and transporting energy from outside the service territory) significant changes in opinion occurred over the period of the deliberations. Before deliberation, renewable energy had been the first choice, but this dropped considerably as support shifted to energy conservation. Interest in renewable energy was not abandoned – in all cases there was a dramatic rise in the number of citizens who were willing to pay extra for more investment in renewables; rather, conservation was seen as a more cost-effective solution. Reflecting on the results of the utility polls, Fishkin argues that they 'highlight the fact that on issues where the public has not invested a lot of time and attention, the changes are likely to be large because the public is arriving at a considered judgement where previous responses would have represented only "top of the head" views or even "nonattitudes" or nonexistent opinions' (Fishkin, 1997: 202).

Citizens' juries have been run and promoted since the 1970s in both Germany (where they are known as planning cells) and the United States, and more recently in the UK (Stewart *et al.*, 1994; Smith and Wales, 1999). It is in Germany that they have had most political impact, with a range of government bodies and agencies commissioning planning cells on a number of different policy issues, such as planning, energy and transport policy, and agreeing to take into account their recommendations in future decisions. The original architects of the process – Peter Dienel and Ned Crosby – have both argued that the model is particularly useful in engaging citizens directly in environmental policy making (Crosby, 1995; Dienel and Renn, 1995). Two citizens' jury experiments in the UK – on the creation of wetlands in the Fens (Aldred and Jacobs, 1997) and waste management in Hertfordshire (Kuper, 1997) – produced recommendations that take environmental concerns more seriously than much existing policy and support the view that citizens are willing and able to deliberate about fairly complex and detailed environmental issues.[8]

Consensus conferences have been run regularly since the 1980s by the Danish Board of Technology as a means of incorporating the perspectives of the lay public within the assessment of new and often controversial scientific and technological developments that raise serious social and ethical concerns. The lay panel's recommendations have no statutory authority, but have sometimes had direct impact on the legislative process in the Danish parliament. For example, the recommendations of the panel on genetic engineering in industry and agriculture led to the exclusion of transgenic animals from the first governmental biotechnology research and development programme (Klüver, 1995: 44). Experiments with consensus conferences have also occurred in The Netherlands, New Zealand, Switzerland and the UK, although without the level of media and public interest or political impact observed in Denmark. The first UK National Consensus Conference (UKNCC) on Plant Biotechnology was held in November 1994, hosted by the Science Museum. It aimed 'to contribute to public debate and policymaking by providing insight into public perception of agricultural and food biotechnology in Britain' (Joss and Durant, 1995: 195). Unfortunately, there was no formal link to the policy process, negligible political or public interest and some criticism at the time from environmentalists about the scope of the question and the choice of witnesses (Purdue, 1996). Even though the report was generally sympathetic to the biotechnology industry, the lay panel recommendations included improved consumer information and labelling and greater monitoring of genetically modified products (UKNCC, 1994), recommendations that the British government would have been wise to consider given the recent public backlash against the technology. The second UKNCC on Radioactive Waste Management took place in May 1999 (Palmer, 1999).[9] Again, environmental interests were not entirely satisfied with the final recommendations, but there was a recognition that they were more sensitive to environmental concerns than existing policy. In an evaluation of consensus conferences, the Royal Commission on Environmental Pollution (RCEP – an advisory body to the UK government) argues:

> The usefulness of consensus conferences can be shown by contrasting UK and Danish experience over food irradiation. The Danish Parliament had available a very negative report by a lay panel and decided that irradiation of food should not be approved for general use. In the UK the Advisory Committee on Novel Foods and Processes decided that the process should be introduced. There was a hostile response from the public, and industry was unable to use plant it had installed. That outcome might well have been avoided if there had been appropriate public debate before the decision was taken.
>
> (RCEP, 1998: 108)

A number of areas of concern remain about the practice of citizen forums, in particular the potential for agenda setting and manipulation of results, the form of selection and representation and the nature of the outcome. Well before any citizen deliberations, the potential for agenda setting and the mobilisation of bias is at its highest, with the selection of the issue to be addressed and the choice of relevant information and witnesses. The independence of the facilitating organisation is fundamental here, and organisers are often fastidious in their attempt to draw together a range of stakeholders to help select relevant questions and evidence. In the consensus conference model, the citizen panel is brought together for preparatory weekends, during which they have the opportunity to be involved in the selection of expert witnesses and key questions. In the citizens' jury process, citizens are typically given the opportunity to call new witnesses as they deliberate and learn about the issues under consideration. The problem of authorities selectively adopting ('cherry-picking') results is somewhat ameliorated in citizens' juries in Germany and the UK, where a pre-jury contract is drawn up between the independent facilitating organisation, the commissioning body and the jurors, requiring the commissioning body either to act on the jury recommendations or to give reasons why it has decided not to act.

There are also concerns with the process of selection. First, random selection is not the same as equality of opportunity to participate in deliberative forums. As Saward suggests, 'the acceptability of this idea (random selection) is far from clear-cut – there is a difference between (1) having an opportunity to participate, and (2) having an opportunity to have an opportunity to participate' (Saward, 2000b: 16). Second, questions are raised as to whether such a small number of participants can be representative of the wider political community. Although some advocates argue that forums aim to realise a 'microcosm' model of representation (Crosby, 1995; Fishkin, 1997), it is important that citizens are not seen as representing 'people like them' in any strong sense. No group of citizens can accurately mirror all the standpoints and views present within the wider community, and there is a danger of creating false essentialisms: an expectation that participants represent the views of citizens who share similar characteristics. But this would be a mistake, as citizens who share similar socio-demographic characteristics do not necessarily share the same views and attitudes. For example, women in these forums should not be seen as representing all women in the wider community. An emphasis on representation may undermine the ideal of active citizenship and the emergence of democratic deliberation. Rather, the legitimacy of citizen forums rests on drawing together a range of citizens who are able to reflect upon a wide variety of experiences and perspectives. The primary task of participating citizens should be understood in terms of *deliberation* rather than *representation* (Smith and Wales, 2000: 56–7). Jeffrey Abramson draws out this point in relation to legal juries:

> We do not want to encourage jurors to see themselves as irreconcilably divided by race, selected only to fill a particular racial or gender slot on the jury. Yet we do want to encourage jurors to draw upon and combine their individual experiences and

group backgrounds in the joint search for the most reliable and accurate verdict. The difference is subtle but real.

(Abramson, 1994: 11)

Finally, citizens may feel pressure to suppress any conflict in order to achieve consensus. This has been recognised by facilitators in citizens' ·juries, who are particularly alert to the way in which articulate and outspoken individuals can dominate the agenda and define a consensus (Smith and Wales, 1999: 303–4). Room is typically made to accommodate differences and disagreement in majority/minority decisions. The problem would appear to be most acute in consensus conferences, as the name suggests. As a project manager from the Danish Board of Technology stresses: 'every effort is made to attain the greatest consensus between the lay-panel members on the actions to be recommended. Minority opinions should be allowed only when the process reveals very wide differences of opinion' (Grundahl, 1995: 37). There is a fine line between the search for consensus and the suppression of conflict.

To a great extent, this problem is avoided in deliberative opinion polls, given that the outcome is the individuals' post-deliberation opinions on a range of questions. Only after the poll are these preferences aggregated and statistically manipulated. In consensus conferences and citizens' juries, concerns are raised about the process of how recommendations are generated, but their strength is that the citizens themselves are collectively engaged in this process and are able to debate and reflect on how their differing opinions and values should be balanced in any recommendations. With deliberative polls, however, it is a third party that aggregates the individual preferences.[10] Though citizens' juries and consensus conferences tell us something about how citizens might balance competing opinions and values, and provide us with clear recommendations, in deliberative opinion polls that job is left to an analyst. Citizens in deliberative opinion polls are less likely to feel any pressure to achieve consensus; however, they are not given the opportunity to exercise the type of political judgement required in coming to collective political decisions (Smith, 2000).

Typically, these experiments have been used at a local or national level. Although, as far as I am aware, no cross-national forums have been run, there is no obvious reason why they could not be used across traditional geographic boundaries, drawing together citizens from within the 'natural' constituency of particular environmental problems and issues. In almost all cases, advocates of these innovations argue they should not be seen as an *alternative* to existing representative structures, but rather as a *complement*; as decision *recommending* rather than decision *taking*. Reviewing recent evidence, the RCEP recommended that methods such as citizens' juries, consensus conferences and deliberative opinion polling should be used to elicit citizens' values when setting environmental standards for 'issues which are both complex or controversial and of broad scope' (RCEP, 1998: 111). At one and the same time, citizen forums are seen as providing decision makers with the informed view of citizens and as responding to the perceived democratic deficit in contemporary society – the growing distance between the lives, experiences and attitudes of citizens and the decisions made in their name.

Model 3: citizen initiative and referendum

Referendum and initiative are two processes by which a population can vote directly on policy issues. Referendums can be advisory or mandatory – in certain countries, laws and constitutional changes require a popular vote. The initiative offers a process through which citizens are able to put forward new legislation or nullify existing laws. Typically, citizens will be required to collect a certain number of signatures to have their suggestion placed on a ballot and put to a popular vote. The extension of direct democracy through the use of referendums and initiatives has been promoted by both Ian Budge (1996; 2001) and Saward (1998a). Budge argues for more direct involvement of citizens within decision making for two reasons: first, given the interval between elections, there is little influence through voting on the policies that governments pursue; and, second, the link between voter preferences and policy packages is tenuous (Budge, 1996: 15). Based on a defence of the core value of political equality, Saward argues that the extended use of referendums and initiatives would maximise responsive rule, defined as 'necessary correspondence between acts of governance and the equally weighted felt interests of citizens with respect to those acts' (Saward, 1998a: 51).

Such a defence of the use of referendums and initiatives ought to be of interest to both greens and deliberative democrats, and it is quite astonishing that they have been little discussed within either literature. For greens, the desire for small-scale, face-to-face forms of democracy means that these typically large-scale mechanisms have generally been ignored; for deliberative democrats, their frequent antipathy towards forms of aggregation appears to have resulted in the same fate. However, unlike the two previous models discussed, the use of referendums and initiatives theoretically fulfils the criterion of inclusiveness or political equality – this is at the heart of Budge and Saward's defence of the institution. Participation is full, unmediated and direct – it is not mediated by group representatives (mediation) or by a sample of citizens (citizen forums). The initiative particularly offers a unique mechanism by which agenda setting by political authorities can be, if not neutralised, at the very least reduced. Drawing on the Swiss use of such mechanisms, Wolf Linder highlights the manner in which the political agenda can be broadened:

> If we sum up the innovating effects of the popular initiative, we can distinguish three facets:
> 1 Initiatives allow *new issues* to be put on the agenda, issues that are either different from the preoccupations of or neglected by the political establishment or the government coalition.
> 2 Initiatives can lead to an *acceleration of institutional processes* when used as a support for innovations desired by the government coalition, such as environmental policy, which Switzerland was to implement earlier than other European countries.
> 3 Initiatives allow *discontent with the establishment* to be expressed which can lead to policy changes inside the government coalition.
>
> (Linder, 1994: 105; also Saward, 1998a: 63)

Inclusiveness is only one aspect of deliberative design. What about the fostering of democratic dialogue? Here, referendums and initiatives might appear weak, especially in comparison with the highly structured environment of citizen forums and mediation. However, as we have already seen, many deliberative theorists celebrate the public sphere of civil society as the location par excellence of democratic deliberation (e.g. Benhabib, 1996; Dryzek, 2000a). If this is the case, referendums, and especially initiatives, offer innovative mechanisms for communicating wider public debate and opinion and affecting decision making. But Simone Chambers is not convinced of the deliberative potential of referendums and initiatives. She believes that the majoritarian decision rule (the yes/no vote) hinders the cultivation of mutuality and reciprocity, dispositions essential to democratic dialogue: 'referendums invite participants to approach debate strategically rather than discursively, that is it creates the incentive to find arguments that will sway only the needed number of voters' (Chambers, 2001: 241). We are faced with the paradox that the use of particular decision rules may undermine the conditions for democratic dialogue. As Chambers notes: 'majoritarianism requires deliberation in order to be legitimate but majority decision rules create disincentives to engage in deliberation, that is to participate as a discursive actor' (ibid.: 244–5). This disincentive might be reduced if referendums and initiatives do not simply lead to binary, all-or-nothing decisions but rather use multi-option ballots and are part of a wider process of consultation or an iterative process in which the issue is returned to after a given period of time (ibid.: 250–1; Barber, 1984: 286).

Referendums and initiatives are frequently criticised on the grounds that citizens lack the competence to make sound judgements about policy and that political, economic and social inequalities within society affect participation and the results of ballots – the manipulative effect of political elites, money and the media being of particular concern. The question of competence has been tackled directly by Thomas Cronin, who places much emphasis on the civic responsibility of citizens. He argues that initiatives and referendums in the United States have generally been used:

> in a reasonable and constructive manner. Voters have been cautious and have almost always rejected extreme proposals. Most studies suggest that voters, despite the complexity of measures and the deceptions of some campaigns, exercise shrewd judgement, and most students of direct democracy believe most American voters take their responsibility seriously.
> (Cronin, 1989: 197; also Budge, 1996: 89; Lupia and Johnston, 2001)

There is some concern that initiatives in particular are more likely to produce outcomes unfavourable to minorities. Although there are a small number of well-documented examples of successful discriminatory initiatives, it appears that voters are more tolerant than critics contend. It is important to compare the decisions made using this mechanism with those passed by legislatures that do not use initiatives: there is no clear evidence that the former leads to less tolerant judgements (Kobach, 1994; Bowler and Donovan, 2001). Either way, the constitutional framework within which direct democratic mechanisms operate is an important consideration in order to protect vulnerable minorities.

The practice of referendums and initiatives certainly suffers from the effects of political, material and social inequalities. In studies of American and Swiss use of referendum, Cronin and Linder both note that middle-aged men with higher incomes and levels of education are more likely to vote (Cronin, 1989; Linder, 1994). As Linder argues: 'The most important restriction on the democratic norm of equal and general participation . . . lies in the unequal representation of social classes' (Linder, 1994: 95). Low participation rates is one problem; but of even more concern is the socially and economically uneven participation rates, a problem that is not exclusive to referendums and initiatives (Parry *et al.*, 1992).

Although the final decision rests in the hands of the citizenry, it is only in the imagination of theorists that political elites step back and leave citizens to deliberate and judge among themselves. Referendums and initiatives are mediated by elites: most obviously in government-sponsored referendums, but also in initiatives. As Matthew Mendelsohn and Andrew Parkin argue: 'The referendum is one device among many used by parties, politicians and interest groups to shape the political agenda, influence political outcomes, resolve internal disputes and alter the political dynamics affecting their interests' (Mendelsohn and Parkin, 2001: 19). Critics view the activities of political elites as undermining the democratic nature of referendums and initiatives; for others, the role of political parties in particular is essential to mobilise voters and provide information (Budge, 1996; 2001; Lupia and Johnston, 2001).

Aggravating this problem further, the recent history of initiatives and referendums also shows the growing influence of money, paid petition circulators, direct mail deception and deceptive advertising campaigns. Given that the deliberative potential of direct voting rests on access to balanced information (Saward, 1998a: 60ff.), the educational and civic claims of advocates is under threat because 'the side with more money too often gets to define the issues and structure the debate in an unbalanced way' (Cronin, 1989: 226). Media manipulation is rife, particularly when business interests are threatened. However, this is a criticism of the existing practice of initiatives and referendums, not of their potential. It means that we need to spend time investigating possible 'imaginative safeguards' to ensure that information is balanced and that the influence of money and media interests does not continue to grow (Cronin, 1989; Saward, 1998a).[11]

Referendums and initiatives on environmental measures have been affected and defeated by large-scale spending by opponents, typically business interests. Often, the issues at stake have been grossly misrepresented through the media. However, even with the imbalance of resources, greens have had success. Cronin, for example, highlights the 1980 Oregon anti-nuclear power initiative as one 'low-budget' victory over high-spending corporate opponents' (Cronin, 1989: 115). Environmental initiatives have generally been successful when there is effective grass-roots organisation and mobilisation in the provision of information. Even with the influence of particular business and media interests, the citizen initiative provides a democratic mechanism through which issues of importance to marginalised groups in the polity can be raised in the public domain. Environmentalists are a good example of such a group and 'have used the initiative process to force legislatures to give greater consideration to conservation and environmental protection issues' (ibid.: 225). Environmental concerns such as nuclear freeze, nuclear-free zones, land use, public utilities, bottle deposits and nuclear power plants have been one of the main subject areas on state ballots. Cronin adds that 'the record suggests that the public can . . . act responsibly. Indeed, on environmental matters the public appears to be more responsible than state legislatures . . . The fear that populist democracy via initiative, referendum, and recall would lead to irresponsible, mercurial, or even bizarre decision making has not been borne out' (ibid.: 231–2).

In Switzerland, greens have used initiatives to raise awareness of environmental and other issues. In the 1970s and 1980s, when traditional parliamentary parties showed little interest, environmental groups used initiatives to place environmental issues firmly on the political agenda. Kris Kobach estimates that approximately one-third of all initiatives submitted were in the areas of environmental protection, nuclear energy limitation and road traffic restrictions (Kobach, 1994: 143). Even when initiatives were not successful, placing the issue on the political agenda forced the government to respond to environmental concerns earlier than in many other liberal democratic nations. Additionally, it provided the opportunity for greens to establish themselves as a national political party, eventually achieving representation in the legislature (Kobach, 1994: 143; Linder, 1994: 105).

Budge argues that greens should be in favour of increased use of initiatives and referendums on the grounds that they widen the political agenda and are 'more likely to overturn established pro-business policy than normal parliamentary proceedings' (Budge, 1996: 87). The initiative is a mechanism by which groups within civil society can 'repeatedly challenge the government to defend the status-quo' (Kobach, 1994: 149). Additionally, the potential civic and educational value of referendums and initiatives should be of interest to theorists who promote the idea of green citizenship.

In terms of scope and scale, referendums and initiatives in principle know no boundaries and could potentially be used on local through to international issues. Transnational referendums are conceivable, although practical questions of isolating the affected population and the effect of differential results across states need to be attended to (Budge, 1996: 168–71; Saward, 1998a: 135–8; Held, 1995: 273). The use of referendums and initiatives offers an innovative solution to developing a form of direct democracy within and across large-scale societies. As Saward argues:

> direct democracy need not . . . be face-to-face democracy; it does not depend upon the capacity of the members of the political unit to gather together in one place to make decisions . . . The key point about referendum is that it can be used regardless of the size of the political unit, in terms of either geographical extension or population size.
>
> (Saward, 1998a: 83)

Contrasting deliberative institutions

> The examples of discursive design that can be brought to bear
> are no doubt sparse and imperfect, but they nonetheless indicate
> that communicative contexts can be designed and developed
> to supply incentives for a significantly better approximation to
> communicative rationality than is usual in policy deliberations.
>
> (Torgerson, 1999: 138)

This initial analysis of three possible models for deliberative political institutions hopefully shows that greens need to be thinking creatively about questions of institutional design. There are conceivable alternative mechanisms for the transmission of public opinion that allow for the articulation of environmental values in a context that supports unconstrained dialogue. None of the three models is perfect; all have different strengths and weaknesses. A brief comparison of the institutional forms in relation to the four broad criteria offered at the beginning of this chapter will begin to shed some light on their relative effectiveness.

Inclusiveness is most obviously achieved at a formal level in referendums and popular votes on initiatives. All citizens have the right to participate, both in voting and in attempting to place their suggestions on a ballot. However, whether this translates into equality of voice in practice is far from obvious. As our analysis highlights, social and economic inequalities affect the procedures in at least two ways: first, who actually votes; and, second, the collection of signatures for initiatives. In contrast, citizen forums and mediation processes compromise inclusiveness, but in different ways. Forums aim to include a cross-section of the population through the use of sampling techniques. Equality of voice for those involved is then achieved through the setting of ground rules by the participants and the attentiveness of the independent facilitators. In mediation and stakeholder processes, inclusiveness is compromised by the use of representation. Mediation does not involve direct citizen engagement, rather representation of citizens' perspectives through groups with an interest in the specific issue at hand. For under-resourced or less well-organised interests, this is problematic. As with citizen forums, the potential for equality of voice for those interests present is high as long as the mediator takes an activist orientation to the proceedings.

Turning to the cultivation of *unconstrained dialogue,* it is probably citizen forums that offer the most conducive environment: deliberations are highly structured to protect against the insidious exercise of power. The relatively small number of participants (which was a weakness in relation to inclusiveness) offers a supportive context for the development of empathy towards the perspectives of other citizens with contrasting views. The facilitator plays an important role in cultivating a conducive ethos for dialogue and judgement. Mediation also involves small numbers, which may offer similar protections and opportunities. One of the interesting features of the design of both citizen forums and mediation that helps protect deliberations is the absence of an audience during periods of dialogue. This throws up a further dilemma for deliberative design. Being away from the pressures of the public gaze means that those involved in the process are likely to be more open to the possibility of transformation. In some ways, though, this could be seen as contradicting the deliberative democratic ideal of free and open deliberation. The need to protect the sphere of deliberation from the pressures of the wider community is in tension with the virtue of publicity. Publicity is at one and the same time a defence against strategic manipulation *and* a potential barrier to participants developing a deliberative disposition.

In contrast, the deliberations that precede voting in referendums and on initiatives are far less structured and more open to strategic abuse. Our analysis highlights the capacity of powerful interests to set the terms of public debate and to affect the provision of information. It is for this reason that advocates such as Cronin and Saward argue for institutional safeguards to protect the fairness of proceedings. In situations in which deliberations take place across the whole polity, there is likely to be far less coherence and there are more opportunities to influence proceedings through insidious forms of rhetoric. On the positive side, however, initiatives offer an innovative mechanism through which citizens can have more impact on setting the agenda of debates, if not their actual content and direction. Agenda setting is a matter of deep concern in the design of all three models: who decides what is and what is not a matter for deliberation? Mediation, citizens' juries and consensus conferences have a *creative* aspect in their design in that the outcome is not predetermined by the choices on a ballot paper (referendums and initiatives) or a questionnaire (deliberative opinion polls). Participants have the opportunity to shape the nature of the final decisions.

Our third area of interest, *decision rules*, throws up some interesting insights for institutional design. The three citizen forums take different approaches. Consensus conferences are just that – they seek to find areas of consensus among participants on controversial issues of technology policy. We have already raised a concern that this may lead to a pressure to conform. This pressure may also be present to a certain extent in citizens' juries, although here, if consensus or a workable solution does not emerge, simple majoritarian voting can take place. As the name suggests, deliberative opinion polls leave the analysis of individual opinions to a third party. Mediation requires at the minimum a workable solution, and here an added strength of the design is that those making the decisions are frequently the actors responsible for implementation. Ownership of the decision is an important factor. Finally, referendums and initiatives end with an aggregation of votes. This need not be based on a simple yes/no; ballots can be quite sophisticated and part of an iterative process whereby citizens return to the issue after a period of time.

The final criterion relates to the sensitivity of the different models to, first, the *plurality of environmental values*; and, second, the *nature of environmental problems*. In all three cases, there is evidence to suggest that they have been relatively sensitive to the perspectives of environmentalists, although they have not always resulted in green outcomes. However, referendums – even if using the multi-option ballot suggested by Benjamin Barber – may lack sensitivity to the complex nature of many environmental problems. On this issue, mediation, citizen juries and consensus conferences, in particular, offer a context in which the complexity and interconnectedness of environmental policy might be creatively explored. Turning to the question of scale, there is potential for all the different mechanisms to be used at the appropriate ecological level rather than being limited to ecologically arbitrary political boundaries. The use of these mechanisms may not always provide the results that greens desire, but there are good reasons for them to participate in these processes and, thus, to afford them democratic legitimacy.

We need to be aware that the analysis of the actual practice of these three possible designs takes place against a political, social and economic backdrop that is far from supportive of meaningful citizen participation. As Forester warns, although 'much of what practitioners write . . . is hype, and often marketing hype, much of what academics write is often insensitive to the demands of practice, the demands to do as well as one can in the present institutional context' (Forester, 1992: 247). As such, any indication that they may have democratic potential merits further investigation. And such indications are present. Thus, the task becomes one of embedding good practice and defending and extending such arenas of democratic innovation.

Conclusion

There is a need to think creatively about how such embedding of deliberative institutions could take place. There is no single 'best' design: different models will be useful in different circumstances, for different purposes, at different levels and on different issues. There is no blueprint. And the three models do not need to be thought of in isolation. There is a potential for them to be combined in creative ways. Saward, who has reservations about citizen forums, argues that there may be an important role for deliberative opinion polls, to set in motion 'in-depth deliberations on proposed initiatives or pieces of government legislation' (Saward, 1998a: 118; cf. Chambers, 2001: 248–52). Suggestions have been made that referendums could be used to both legitimate and ratify decisions from mediation processes and to make them legally binding (Sullivan, in Susskind and Ozawa, 1995: 150). And stakeholder forums are often established to set the agenda for citizen forums such as citizen juries (Smith and Wales, 1999). What is clear is that citizens can be more deeply engaged in the policy process in ways that enhance deliberation, mutual understanding and the consideration of environmental values. The message of this analysis is surely that greens should begin to think both imaginatively and practically about the question of institutional design. We continue that task in the next chapter, as our attention moves from these mechanisms of transmission of public opinion to the broader context of ecological democratisation.

5 Towards ecological democratisation

The central argument running through this book has been that, in order to do justice to the plurality of environmental (and non-environmental) values and commitments of citizens, decision-making processes ought to promote and enhance democratic deliberation. Particular attention has been paid to the analysis of possible mechanisms of transmission of public opinion, specifically mediation, citizen forums, and referendums and citizen initiatives. The aim has been to show that there are feasible alternative designs to the appraisal techniques, such as CBA, that are widely used in contemporary liberal democratic institutions.

This final chapter aims to broaden the analysis to the possibility of a wider project of 'ecological democratisation'. Mediation, citizen forums, initiatives and referendums have distinct roles to play in linking public opinion to decision-making processes. However, their implementation should not be understood as the only type of institutional change that is possible in contemporary polities. In this chapter, our speculative analysis will centre on three other locations fundamental to the development of a green democratic polity: the constitution; representative legislative assemblies; and civil society. All three areas of analysis have received recent attention within green political theory. To what extent might these locations of political engagement be enhanced in order to embed more deeply democratic deliberation and consideration of environmental values?

Constitutional environmentalism[1]

Our interest in the constitution is twofold. First, to what extent can the constitution legitimately be used to protect the environment and promote environmental sustainability? Second, to what extent can it promote democratic deliberation and reflection on the plurality of environmental values?

The Brundtland Commission's primary legal proposal in its report, *Our Common Future,* is an environmental right of the form: 'All human beings have the fundamental right to an environment adequate for their health and well being' (World Commission on Environment and Development, 1987: 348). Although in the intervening years a significant number of states have entrenched environmental rights within their constitutions (Hayward, 1998: 178), until relatively recently there has been a lack of attention given to the environmental aspects of constitutions within green political theory. This lack of attention is surprising, since, as Robyn Eckersley argues: 'The introduction of environmental rights clearly has the potential to alter radically the established framework of decision making in favour of "the environment"' (Eckersley, 1996: 216). Greens ought to be interested in the structure of the constitution, because the impact of rights is felt across moral, political and legal spheres.

A number of different arguments have been employed for securing environmental rights. Eckersley summarises the ecological challenge to liberal conceptions of rights by arguing that the liberal defence of the moral priority of autonomy and protection from domination requires attention to the material conditions of its exercise: 'we must accord the same moral priority to the material conditions (including bodily and ecological conditions) that enable that autonomy to be exercised' (Eckersley, 1996: 223). As Ted Benton argues, our organic well-being (or 'embodiment') is dependent on the protection of the ecological conditions of life:

> humans, as living organisms, depend for their organic well-being on their (socially mediated) relation to their ecological conditions of life. If such basic requirements can ground rights . . . then we are led to postulate appropriate environmental conditions for organic well-being as itself a right which ought to be considered alongside, and presupposed by the rights to freedom of worship, of speech and so on.
>
> (Benton, 1993: 175)

Benton's socialist-inspired critique of the individualism inherent within the liberal rights discourse leads him to argue that such an environmental right would require 'the preservation of the ecological integrity of a sufficient geographical terrain' suitable to sustaining the social life, which itself sustains well-being (ibid.). Thus, he is able to develop a sophisticated rights-based critique of development strategies and practices that threaten and undermine the traditional ways of life of indigenous peoples.

John Dryzek offers a similar argument about necessary ecological preconditions: 'the human-life support capacity of natural systems is *the* generalisable interest *par excellence*, standing as it does in logical antecedence to competing normative principles such as utility maximisation or right protection' (Dryzek, 1987: 204).[2] An environmental right to a functioning ecosystem is a necessary (although not sufficient) condition for a functioning democratic polity.

Michael Saward offers a different approach, arguing that environmental rights are inextricably linked to fundamental democratic rights to social provision. He is particularly concerned that the right to adequate health care is undermined by *preventable* environmental risks. Examples here would include the risk of harm caused by proximity to nuclear facilities, urban traffic pollution, etc. Saward contends: 'In order to exercise their basic rights and freedoms in the face of a certain class of preventable risks, citizens of democracy have, on the face of it, a claim to a green democratic right not to suffer certain consequences that would flow from the actualisation of such risk' (Saward, 1996: 88).[3]

The existence of substantive environmental rights returns us to arguments initially raised in Chapter 3. Robert Goodin (1992) famously warned greens that there is a tension between democracy and ecological principles and values. However, the arguments above suggest that environmental rights and certain fundamental democratic rights are actually inextricably connected. As Saward argues: 'Rather than being something *outside* the purview of democratic theory, core environmental concerns are part of it' (Saward, 1996: 88; also Hayward, 1998: 161).

For many greens, the nature of the rights discussed above reflect only a minimal understanding of environmental values. Arguments have been offered which extend the scope of environmental rights beyond immediate threats to human health and well-being. As Tim Hayward recognises, 'depending on how health and, particularly, well-being are construed, many other issues could ultimately be brought under this rubric including aspects of environmental concern that touch on the quality of life in aesthetic, cultural and spiritual terms' (Hayward, 2000: 559). Just such an approach is taken by Benton, who argues for a broader conception of well-being that requires sensitivity to the 'cultural dislocation and loss of identity involved in ecological destruction ... the distinctively cultural, symbolic aspect or moment in human/environmental relationships'. Such a recognition, he believes, will 'strengthen and enrich the case for environmental rights' (Benton, 1993: 177). This conception of human well-being resembles features of the more environmentally sensitive (or weak) anthropocentrism offered in Chapter 1, and more effectively reflects the plurality of environmental values. While recognising the importance of the protection of an enriched sense of well-being, attempts to establish broader environmental rights may be controversial and problematic. In Chapter 1, we recognised that, beyond the necessary biological conditions for life, there is a range of environmental values – use, aesthetic, scientific, cultural, spiritual, etc. – that can be constitutive of well-being. These values can conflict. An expanded substantive right may privilege certain environmental values, at the same time marginalising others. We thus need to be careful how such a right is to be articulated.

Both Benton and Eckersley, among others, wish to move beyond what remains a focus on *human* environmental rights. The status of non-human animals has become a much debated and highly controversial subject within green politics, and Benton's (1993) argument for the consideration of animal rights draws on the continuity between humans and non-human animals in terms of health and bodily integrity and environmental embeddedness.[4] Developing this line of argument further, Eckersley contends that a broader defence of respect for the autonomy of *all* life-forms might form the basis of a reformulated rights discourse. If successful, this would also 'serve as a linchpin between ecocentric values and democracy' (Eckersley, 1995: 173). Eckersley's aim is to develop a rights discourse that respects and protects the right of environmental entities, including species and ecosystems, to unfold in their own ways. However, although she believes that it is possible to reformulate the rights discourse to include individual organisms and classes of organisms,[5] 'the challenge of fashioning an ecocentric rights discourse increases exponentially as we move from a consideration of individual organisms, and classes of organisms, to systematic entities such as ecosystems'. Here we encounter ontological dilemmas: problems of boundary definition that we initially recognised in Chapter 1. As Eckersley continues: 'it is no easy matter to determine the boundaries of ecosystems or other collective entities *with the degree of precision that would be required for the purposes of rights ascription*' (ibid.: 190).

The theoretical move to include non-human animals (Benton, 1993) and then individual organisms, populations and species (Eckersley, 1995) within constitutional environmental rights is certainly controversial. Eckersley recognises that any further attempt to move beyond this point to the wider biotic community would make the rights discourse 'strained and unworkable, morally, politically and legally' (ibid.: 193). However, this criticism can also be levelled at both Benton's and Eckersley's existing proposals. Their conceptions of non-human rights may themselves strain the discourse both in principle and practice, particularly when we consider the plurality of competing claims that are likely to emerge and the negative effect this would likely have on the widespread public support and understanding of rights (Hayward, 1998: 159). The first step, then, for the project of constitutional environmentalism must surely be to ensure the entrenchment of *human* environmental rights. These appear relatively uncontroversial. Stretching the discourse to classes of non-human animals and beyond is a more controversial and questionable step.

However, even if we are to focus simply on human environmental rights, we are still left with two important question. First, what is the substantive content of such a right? And, second, how are we to ensure enforcement? To begin with the substantive content of environmental rights, we have already seen that the nature of 'well being' can be broadened to include issues of environmental and cultural identity. Returning to the Brundtland proposal, we are thus left with a question of what constitutes an 'adequate environment'. To a certain extent, this is going to be culturally sensitive. As Benton recognises, 'there is a case for regarding some set of environmental conditions of well-being as valid objects of universal human rights claims, although the concrete content of these claims cannot be established independently both of some specification of the material culture of those on behalf of whom the claim is made and of the bio-physical sustaining conditions of that culture' (Benton, 1993: 178). Endemic scientific uncertainty about the carrying capacity of ecosystems simply reinforces the problem.

Eckersley offers one possible answer to this problem by arguing that instead of 'an abstract, ambiguous "right to clean air and water", an environmental bill of rights (whether embodied in ordinary legislation or the constitution) might declare, say, that citizens have a right to ensure that environmental quality is maintained in accordance with the standards set by current environmental laws (standards which would undergo regular public review)' (Eckersley, 1996: 230). This formulation has a number of merits. It would allow the substantive content of any right to be the subject of continual debate and deliberation, thus allowing reflection on the tensions between different environmental and non-environmental values. Ongoing consideration is particularly important if we wish to move beyond the right to have a functioning environment adequate for life support, to a more positive (and thus controversial) conception of environmental rights that includes, for example, the protection of the environment for aesthetic, cultural and other purposes. Eckersley's last comment about 'public review' is crucial because it points to the importance that green theorists place not only on substantive environmental rights but also the entrenchment of procedural environmental rights that might ensure enforcement. The range of procedural rights could include rights to information, rights of legal redress and rights of participation (Eckersley, 1996: 230–2; Hayward, 1998: 154–6; 2000: 563). What is particularly pertinent about these procedural rights is that they offer conditions for the establishment and protection of democratic deliberation and the facilitation of the practice of ecological citizenship in the formulation, enforcement and evaluation of environmental policy. Democratic deliberation cannot effectively progress without adequate environmental information, much of which is held by public and private authorities. Legal redress offers the opportunity to object to decisions and actions of public and private bodies that contravene environmental rights and law. Thus, environmental law acts as a legitimate constraint on the outcomes of democratic policy making. But, given the right to participation, the content of environmental policy, standards and law itself becomes a legitimate subject of democratic deliberation. As Eckersley argues:

'Such procedural safeguards would not only help to redress the current under-representation of environmental interests but would also provide a firmer guarantee of environmental decision making according to law – thereby redressing the pervasive "implementation deficit" in environmental law and administration' (Eckersley, 1996: 230).

The important connection between substantive and procedural environmental rights was recognised in 1998 by the member states of the regional United Nations Economic Commission for Europe (UNECE) when they signed the Convention on Access to Information, Public Participation in Decision-making and Access to Justice in Environmental Matters, otherwise known as the Aarhus Convention. This Convention explicitly draws on Principle 10 of the Rio Declaration on Environment and Development (1992), which stresses that transparency, public participation and access to justice are preconditions for achieving sustainable development. The Convention recognises the substantive environmental right 'that every person has the right to live in an environment adequate to his or her health and well-being, and the duty, both individually and in association with others, to protect and improve the environment for the benefit of present and future generations'. However, the primary focus of the Aarhus Convention is on how this right and duty might be exercised. It not only recognises that 'citizens must have access to information, be entitled to participate in decision-making and have access to justice in environmental matters', but also acknowledges that 'citizens may need assistance in order to exercise their rights'. Enhancing the transparency and accountability of public authorities is seen as fundamental; equally, the capacity of institutions to promote participation needs to be developed. In line with the arguments offered in this book, the Convention argues that environmental benefits will flow from increased participation:

> in the field of the environment, improved access to information and public participation in decision-making enhance the quality and the implementation of decisions, contribute to public awareness of environmental issues, give the public the opportunity to express its concerns and enable public authorities to take due account of such concerns.

The Aarhus Convention came into force in October 2001, and the first meeting of the parties took place in October 2002. It is unclear how much force the Convention will have in practice, although Kofi Annan, the UN Secretary General, argues that: 'The Aarhus Convention is the most ambitious venture in environmental democracy undertaken under the auspices of the United Nations. Its adoption was a remarkable step forward in the development of international law' (DEFRA, 2002: 133).[6]

Hayward warns that procedural rights, in particular to participation in decision making, 'are usually exercised by particular interest groups whose claim to represent the "public interest" is always open to legitimate contestation' (Hayward, 2000: 563). The importance of the Aarhus Convention is that it recognises this danger and stresses the important role that political institutions must play in ensuring that this right is exercised in a fair and free manner. To ensure broader and fairer forms of participation, the types of deliberative institutions discussed in Chapter 4 offer potential mechanisms for engaging the wider public. Eckersley recognises that an informed and legally empowered citizenry is perhaps the most important aspect of ecological democratisation, but that the conditions for the emergence and support of such ecologically active citizenship is likely to require the establishment and proper resourcing of an independent Environmental Defenders Office to ensure fair and systematic attention to environmental problems (Eckersley, 1995: 193; 1996: 231; 2000: 130).

Again, Eckersley has also suggested a different kind of procedural constitutional mechanism to ensure the enforcement of substantive environmental rights: the constitutional entrenchment of the precautionary principle (Eckersley, 2000: 129–30). Principle 15 of the Rio Declaration (1992) defines the precautionary principle in the following widely accepted way: 'Where there are threats of serious or irreversible damage, lack of full scientific certainty should not be used as a reason for postponing cost-effective measures to present environmental degradation'. Given the condition of uncertainty and risk surrounding many environmental interventions, reasonable evidence of potential damage, rather than absolute scientific proof, is enough to require the protection of environmental rights (Saward, 1996: 88). The principle would act as a procedural norm in the policy-making process and would also benefit citizens seeking legal redress (one of the suggested procedural rights) against decisions that generate serious potential environmental risk, because the burden of proof would be on the defendant to show why preventative action is not necessary (Eckersley, 1996: 232). Eckersley argues that the constitutional entrenchment of the precautionary principle 'would provide a highly effective and parsimonious means of forcing more systematic consideration of potential environmental impacts on differentially-situated others, including impacts on future generations and non-human species' (Eckersley, 2000: 129).[7] However, even if the principle were not constitutionally embedded, the entrenchment of substantive environmental rights offers strong grounds for the institutionalisation of such a principle in policy making (Hayward, 1998: 156).

We can thus see emerging a vision of an environmentally sensitive constitution which involves the entrenchment of both substantive and procedural environmental rights and norms. This combination has the effect of supporting the institutionalisation of democratic deliberation and responding to some of the fears of critics of deliberation. Substantive environmental rights act as a (sustainability) constraint on the nature of outcomes of deliberations; procedural environmental rights legitimise the development of inclusive democratic dialogue and ecological citizenship and ongoing reflection on the content of any environmental right;[8] and the procedural norm, the precautionary principle, offers the opportunity to direct policy deliberations in more sustainable directions.

Greening representative assemblies

Representative government has a number of defining features including election of representatives at regular intervals, partial independence for those representatives, freedom of public opinion and decisions made after trial by discussion in the assembly of representatives (Manin, 1997: 161ff.). As we have already argued earlier in this book, actually existing representative assemblies have been widely criticised for failing to effectively attend to environmental values and concerns. An influential stream of thought within green political theory views existing representative institutions as fatally flawed and argues for decentralised, self-sufficient communities, typically with face-to-face, directly democratic forms of decision making. However, it is a reasonable assumption that liberal democratic states will remain significant political actors in the foreseeable future, and thus we need to consider the greening of representative assemblies. To a certain extent, the institutionalisation of a strong federal system (with effective representative assemblies as different levels) may begin to appease greens who argue for decentralisation: decision making can then be promoted at the appropriate ecological level and 'provide more points of access for individuals and organised interests, and bring decision-making closer to people's attachment to particular physical spaces' (Saward, 1998b: 351–2). A number of suggestions have emerged as to how elected representative assemblies might be reformed in order to more adequately reflect the plurality of environmental values.[9] Here, we will consider both relatively simple reforms to electoral systems to increase the range of parties represented in the legislature, including green parties, and more radical and controversial suggestions such as the institutionalisation of proxy-representation of future generations and (aspects of) non-human nature. Towards the end of this section, we will also briefly consider proposals to alter the nature and role of representative assemblies, drawing on the three deliberative models discussed in the previous chapter.

Although theorists do not always make the connection themselves, we can understand the arguments about representation within green political theory as following a similar logic to feminist difference theorists, whose concern is with ensuring 'voice' and 'presence' for marginalised groups, such as women and minority ethnic groups, within the political process (Young, 1990b; Phillips, 1995; Squires, 1999; Williams, 2000). Without presence in legislative assemblies and the decision-making process, it is argued, the interests and perspectives of such groups are systematically excluded, or at least not adequately addressed: 'when policies are worked out *for* rather than *with* a politically excluded constituency, they are unlikely to engage all relevant concerns' (Phillips, 1995: 13). The work of difference theorists certainly resonates with the demands of the environmental justice movement in the United States, which bases its critique of existing political decision-making processes on their lack of reflection on the environmental concerns and values of marginalised groups (Schlosberg, 1999). Increasing the representation of marginalised groups would allow the environmental voices of the presently disenfranchised to be heard. Difference can be seen as a 'resource' that helps stimulate deliberations among representatives who reflect the diversity of environmental values.

Empirically, proportional electoral systems have been more favourable to green, women and ethnic minority candidates. The difference theorist Anne Phillips has shown particular interest in proportional systems based on multi-member constituencies allied to a system of cumulative voting (Phillips, 1995). Such a proposal provides citizens with a plurality of votes that they can either concentrate on one candidate or divide among a number. Feminists particularly support the ability to concentrate votes, thus increasing the opportunity of electing candidates from minority communities. From a value pluralist perspective, there are at least three grounds for supporting such an electoral proposal. First, the votes of citizens are more likely to reflect their values and commitments. Cumulative voting allows citizens to spread their votes across different candidates in a way that best corresponds to their values and commitments.[10] Second, given the ability to concentrate votes, one of the parties that is likely to increase its share of the vote is the green party, increasing the likelihood that a specifically environmental voice will be present in the assembly. Third, the overall composition of the legislature is likely to be more heterogeneous and thus better reflect both the diversity of experiences of the non-human world and perspectives on the plurality of environmental values. After all, greens do not have the monopoly on understanding and experiencing the non-human world. This overlap of interest in increasing the diversity of political representatives offers encouraging grounds for integrating the theoretical and practical projects of feminists and environmentalists.[11]

Representing nature

Beyond simple changes to the electoral system, difference feminists have argued for more radical changes that would not just increase the likelihood of, but actually guarantee, representation for women and ethnic minority communities. As Iris Marion Young argues: 'a democratic public should provide mechanisms for the effective recognition and representation of distinct voices and perspectives of those of its constituent groups that are oppressed or disadvantaged' (Young, 1990b: 184). According to Young, oppressed groups are social groups, rather than interest or ideological groups (ibid.: 186; see Squires, 2000: 98–100). Given the level of oppression and disadvantage suffered by such social groups, group representation requires institutional mechanisms and public resources to support self-organisation and self-empowerment,[12] to ensure that policy proposals are considered by decision makers, and, most controversially, to allow veto power over proposals that directly affect the group (Young, 1990b: 184). Sympathetic critics have raised concerns that, given the heterogeneity of contemporary societies and the (internal) heterogeneity of groups themselves, the representative system would be structurally incapable of providing all social groups with institutional voice (Gargarella, 1998: 271) and that, if all disadvantaged groups had the power of veto, the possibility of political deadlock in decision-making processes might be unbearable (Dryzek, 2000a: 61).

Certain green theorists take this difference argument even further, to include the guaranteed representation of 'environmental constituencies', in particular future generations and non-human nature.[13] As Mike Mills argues: 'This type of representational diversity is essential to green political theory and to the programmes of green groups and parties. It targets the democratic process as the mechanism which is, at present, failing to protect the vulnerable and unrepresented' (Mills, 1996: 111). However, the institutional mechanisms suggested by Young cannot be directly extended into the environmental realm for a number of reasons. First it is far from clear that environmental constituencies could be seen as a social group who have suffered the forms of oppression that Young highlights (Young, 1990b: 39ff.). Second, neither future generations nor non-human nature can 'self-organise' or be 'self-empowered' – they cannot articulate their interests and perspectives. If representation is going to occur, it will need to be in the form of a 'proxy'. And this is just what green theorists have suggested (Kavka and Warren, 1983; Dobson, 1996b; Mills, 1996).

It is argued that representation of environmental constituencies can take place, because, although it is not possible for representatives to take instructions or be authorised by the specific constituency, representatives will have a reasonable understanding of the interests of future generations and non-human nature (Kavka and Warren, 1983: 25; Dobson, 1996b: 137). A number of seats would be set aside for representatives of environmental constituencies, who would then sit alongside present generation representatives in the legislative assembly.

But as Andrew Dobson asks: 'Who would comprise the proxy electorate?' (Dobson, 1996b: 132). After all, future generations and non-human nature cannot choose their own representatives. Dobson considers and rejects the idea of an electorate based on a random sample of voters from the present generation on the grounds that there is no guarantee that the interests of future generations and non-human nature would actually be represented within the sample (ibid.: 133). His favoured option is that the proxy-representatives for both future generations and non-human nature ought to be elected from an electorate comprising the sustainability lobby which has internalised the interests of the environmental constituency. To ensure that some citizens do not have two votes, this lobby would be deprived of a vote for candidates representing the present generation and then choose to vote for a representative of either future generations or non-human nature (ibid.: 133–4).

This formulation raises a number of questions that cluster around the lack of authorisation implicit in such a conception of representation. Not only do we have proxy-representation – itself problematic – but also a highly restricted proxy-electorate. Why should such voting be restricted to the sustainability lobby? As we have already argued, greens do not have a monopoly on the plurality of environmental values. Mills offers an alternative approach that mirrors one of Phillips' suggestions discussed earlier: 'multi-member constituencies in which some of the representatives were expected to represent the interests of their non-human constituency members' (Mills, 1996: 110). It is not clear from this formulation whether citizens would have a plurality of votes and whether a certain number of these would have to be placed against representatives of environmental constituencies.[14] But even with a broader (proxy) electorate we are still left with the problem of proxy-authorisation. The appropriateness of such arrangements can be challenged on the simple grounds that future generations and non-human nature 'cannot themselves express and publicly defend their interests' (Barry, 1999: 221). Instead, we have a situation of potential proxy-representatives offering competing perspectives on what these interests may or may not be. This connects with the second type of problem that such proxy-representation raises, namely how are the conflicting interests within these two classes of interests to be represented? It is the heterogeneity problem faced by difference theorists, but taken to greater extremes.[15] The idea of proxy-representatives elected by a proxy-electorate (whatever form it takes) (doubly) undermines the idea of authorisation implicit within the principle of representation as practised in liberal democratic states. It appears both theoretically and practically unsustainable. Young's argument for guaranteed representation for oppressed social groups has proved controversial; the more radical argument for representation of environmental constituencies is even less compelling.

The argument for proxy-representation of 'environmental constituencies' rests on the grounds that existing political representatives do not reflect in enough depth on such interests in democratic decision-making processes. This may be the case, but it is unclear that the answer lies in extending representation in the manner suggested. The type of representation of environmental constituencies that Dobson, Mills and others have argued for is surely already provided by green parties: it is the nature of the electoral system that is the more obvious and feasible target of criticism in nations where they are not present in legislative assemblies. Further, John Barry argues: 'In many respects the argument for the democratic representation of the interests of non-humans ... is a reflection of the failure of these interests to be reflected within the interests of citizens. In other words, the creation of democratic institutions to represent non-human interests arises partly from the lack of "green citizenship" and a wider ecological culture' (Barry, 1999: 22). If political representatives do not perceive an interest in environmental issues among their constituents, then they are unlikely to reflect environmental values in decision-making processes. Part of the argument in the last chapter was that the institutionalisation of deliberative mechanisms for the transmission of public opinion would play a part in altering this situation. And, as Barry contends, the problem may be better located in the development of an ecological culture rather than in altering the representative principle. Again, Eckersley argues that, although the analysis of the problem is correct, a constitutional response may be more practical: 'A procedural norm such as the precautionary principle would appear to be a more parsimonious means of representing nature than providing proxy representation of non-human nature in legislative chambers' (Eckersley, 1999: 46). Both Barry and Eckersley are reminding us that we need to be sensitive to the variety of institutional locations and how they influence and affect one another.

There is a further general problem relating to the reform of practices of representation in legislative assemblies. Our discussions have been concerned with increasing the diversity of experiences of, and perspectives on, the non-human world within assemblies. But voice is only one (although crucial) aspect of democratic deliberation. As we suggested in the introduction of this section on assemblies, one of the defining characteristics of representative government is the principle that decisions are made after trial by discussion within an assembly of representatives (Manin, 1997: 183–92). But is trial by discussion in representative assemblies deliberative in the sense that we have been employing the term?

There are a number of characteristics of representative assemblies that may undermine the deliberative quality of debates.[16] First, the size of assemblies may affect the nature of discussions. Jon Elster argues that, in larger assemblies, dialogue tends to be unsystematic and lack coherence, 'dominated by a small number of skilled and charismatic speakers ... who count on rhetoric rather than argument' (Elster, 1998: 107). This is not to argue that democratic deliberation can only occur in highly structured small group settings (such as citizen forums or mediation processes), but it does raise the question of how deliberation might be institutionalised, protected and enhanced in assemblies. One proposal that could well help increase the consideration of environmental values and ideas in policy debates is the presence of a well-resourced environmental audit committee (supported by, for example, an environmental audit commission or the kind of environmental defender and advocacy organisation suggested by Eckersley) with the ability to scrutinise policy proposals and call witnesses. Second, the publicity of debates within assemblies may have both positive and negative effects. On the positive side, publicity makes it difficult for representatives to appear to be motivated merely by self-interest (ibid.: 111). The presence of an audience may have the moralising effect hoped for by deliberative theorists (Miller, 1992: 61). However, it may also be the case that publicity can make it more difficult for representatives to back down from publicly stated positions: 'It makes it less likely that speakers will change their mind as a result of reasoned objections' (Elster, 1998: 111).

This last problem relates to the relationship between representatives and their constituents and political party. The image of 'deliberative' representatives is one in which representatives put forward arguments based on the interests of their constituents, reflect on the perspectives offered by other representatives and judge in terms of the public good. Transformation of initial preferences is likely in such a process. The reality of the practice of representation is far from this. Representatives are constrained by the interests of their constituents (or at least those whose vote the representative is interested in) and, most obviously, by party allegiance. Representatives who transform their judgements on issues may find themselves in conflict with the (often unreflective) views of their electorate and party, and thus in electoral trouble. The highly partisan and conflictual politics of many legislative assemblies limits the possibility of transformation and appears to undermine their deliberative potential. Such pressures may be lessened under more proportional systems, but only relatively. Similar tensions may well exist between the idea of group representation offered by difference theorists and the requirements within deliberative democracy for representatives to be open to the possibility of transformation (Rosenblum, 1998: 343–6). Those involved in the debate will have to explain to their constituents, who were not necessarily party to deliberations, why their position has changed. Questions remain as to how best to promote and cultivate empathy and enlarged mentality in representative assemblies.

Alternative deliberative designs

We have already drawn some lessons from the institutional designs discussed in Chapter 4. But it may be that we can draw inspiration from these mechanisms to see how assemblies might be reformed, or perhaps restructured and replaced, in an attempt to enhance deliberation and to ensure that the plurality of environmental values are considered in the framing of legislation and policy. Taking the mediation model first, the institutionalisation of stakeholders in decision-making processes could take the form of associative democracy. The ecological potential of such arrangements has been recognised within green political theory (Achterberg, 1996a,b). Theories of associative democracy take two broad approaches: Joshua Cohen and Joel Rogers have argued that the state could actively enhance the capacity of secondary associations to positively affect governance (Cohen and Rogers, 1995); Paul Hirst has offered a more 'bottom-up' approach, with the emergence of a self-governing civil society which takes on many of the activities of the state (Hirst, 1994; 1997).

It is the Cohen and Rogers model that is of most interest here as it views the state (and hence the representative legislative assembly) as playing the primary role in governance, remedying inequalities in representation through state promotion of the organisation of marginalised and disadvantaged groups. Although Cohen and Rogers are predominantly interested in economic associations, in particular the relative inequalities between capital and labour, environmental associations could have a particularly positive impact on the formulation, implementation and evaluation of environmental policy through, for example, the provision of information to establish standards, and ensuring compliance and enforcement (Achterberg, 1996a: 181). By moving beyond economic interests, the model of associative democracy becomes a form of 'inclusive corporatism' (Dryzek, 2000a: 90–1). We noted in the last chapter that there is some evidence that existing state-sponsored corporatist arrangements have been more effective in achieving environmental policy outcomes, and that it is 'the state model most conducive to discursive and democratic civil society' (ibid.: 106–7). Young has argued that a broader notion of associative democracy has resonances with her arguments for institutionalised group representation to ensure oppressed or disadvantaged groups gain 'an equal voice in agenda setting and political formation' (Young, 1995: 212). In the hands of advocates, Cohen and Rogers's model of associative democracy offers potential for increased opportunities for citizen participation within associations and groups and hence within the decision-making process itself (Perczynski, 2000).

But concerns about this approach to associative democracy, and forms of group representation in general, remain. The first reflects uneasiness about possible tensions between representation and democratic deliberation. We have already raised some initial thoughts about this issue in this chapter and in Chapter 4 in relation to mediation. Cohen and Rogers's, and Young's, formulations depend on associations and groups being internally democratic and inclusive such that deliberation will take place not only between representatives but also between representatives and their group members. But, in practice, very few associations even approach this requirement (Roßteutscher, 2000), again raising questions about whether representatives will be constrained in their ability to enter into deliberative exchanges (Mansbridge, 1995: 143–4; M. Williams, 2000). Associative democrats, difference theorists and deliberative democrats wish to ensure voice and presence for all perspectives, especially those of the politically disenfranchised, but would group representatives have the freedom or desire to engage deliberatively? Representing the perspective and interests of a social group or association and being able or even willing to enter into a deliberative process may be in dynamic tension (Smith, 2000: 34–5; Sunstein, 2002).

The second concern with forms of governance directly involving associations is the potentially corrosive effect that such arrangements might have on the vitality of civil society. As Dryzek warns, we need to recognise that 'pressures and movements for democratisation almost always originate in insurgency in civil society rather than the state, a flourishing oppositional civil society is the key to further democratisation'. A truly inclusive state that incorporated a wide variety of voluntary associations may, paradoxically, 'corrode the discursive vitality of civil society . . . and so undermine the conditions for further democratisation' (Dryzek, 2000a: 113–4).

Before we move on to the status and role of civil society within green political theory, it is worth reflecting on the possible extension of the two other models discussed in the previous chapter: citizen forums and referendums and initiatives. Both of these designs promote *direct* citizen engagement and offer insights into alternative designs for legislative and decision-making assemblies.

Given the nature of the outcome of deliberative opinion polls, only citizens' juries and consensus conferences could realistically be extended to become decision-making bodies in their own right. We would thus see our modern understanding of the representative principle replaced by the idea of statistical representation through random sampling or the use of lot. This would be utilised in tandem with rotation for positions of authority: specified time periods after which those in authority would return to the citizen body. Lot and rotation have an impressive political heritage although their use has diminished (Goodwin, 1992; Manin, 1997). An assembly comprising citizens chosen by lot would probably increase the variety of experiences and perspectives on the non-human world and potentially overcome the tensions we have been discussing in relation to representation and deliberation. It would also undermine the strategic influence of political parties and the corrosive effect of the existence of a political class that separates the lives, experiences and perspectives of citizens and professional politicians (Offe and Preuss, 1991: 165).[17] Rotation, importantly, reduces the scope for long-term strategic action and reinforces the principle that citizens both make the law and are subject to its strictures. Legislative and decision-making assemblies created by lot and rotation would certainly offer a radically different political division of labour in contemporary societies.

The most systematic and far-reaching attempt to develop a model of a political system based on statistical representation is undoubtedly John Burnheim's vision of 'demarchy' (Burnheim, 1985). Burnheim proposes that political authorities chosen by a form of lot and rotation would replace the contemporary state. These authorities would have a number of specific features. First they would operate functionally, focusing on specific policy issues such as environment, industrial development, housing, etc. Second, they would vary in geographical scope and coverage. The reach of political authority would reflect the ecological principle of appropriate scale. Third, citizens would be chosen from among individuals with a material interest in the particular functional area.

There are, unsurprisingly, a number of concerns inherent with such a proposal, some specific to Burnheim's demarchy, others more generally related to the principle of lot and rotation. Burnheim's vision of functional authority removes one problem: the ecologically inappropriate geographical coverage of the state. However, it raises another: identifying distinct functions and ensuring coordination between them. For example, attempting to distinguish between issues such as energy, environment and population would be highly problematic (Dryzek, 2000a: 117). Second, citizens are to be chosen from only those with a material interest in the specific functional issue area. This is different from the principle underlying citizen forums, whereby any citizen might be chosen (although with the option of declining the opportunity). The requirement of a material interest may undermine some of the deliberative and transformative potential by introducing a sense of representation into the process: those chosen may see themselves as representing a particular material interest, thus again raising the possibility of tensions between representation and deliberation.

Where assemblies based on lot and rotation raise a more general problem is in relation to our contemporary commitment to direct political accountability and authorisation, implicit within the traditional representative principle. At present, accountability and authorisation are (theoretically) secured through periodic elections. Replacing elections with lot and rotation would mean that citizens no longer choose their representatives. Unexpectedly, the removal of this central tenet of contemporary democratic theory and practice may actually increase the deliberative potential and capacity of assemblies to reflect on the plurality of environmental values. Members of the legislature would no longer be constrained by political party or the electorate within a particular constituency and, in theory, would be more willing to engage in deliberative exchanges and reconsider their perspectives on environmental (and other) values. Whether greens (and others) are willing to trust a random sample of their fellow citizens with political decision making remains an interesting question.

The third model discussed in Chapter 4 was referendum and initiative. Both Ian Budge (1996) and Saward (1998a) have argued that the use of these mechanisms could be extended to create a 'party-based direct democracy'. This vision of direct democracy has two distinct advantages over the type of unmediated forms of direct democracy typically associated with green politics. First, it is applicable to large-scale complex societies. Second, it does not wish away the existence of political parties. The key to the proposal is that assemblies are elected in the same way as present (based on a form of proportional representation), but all legislative decisions are taken by popular referendum with proposals suggested either by the majority party or by citizens through the use of the initiative. Neither Budge nor Saward argues for this proposal on the grounds that it will enhance democratic deliberation; rather it is to ensure responsive rule (Saward, 1998a: 51).

However, from a deliberative perspective, there are a number of interesting features about this novel proposal, in particular the celebration of the role played by political parties in mobilising and coordinating citizens and debates. Cohen explicitly commends the potential of publicly financed political parties to create spaces and forums for democratic deliberation. First, the public funding of political parties frees them from 'the dominance of private resources', thus helping 'to overcome the inequalities in deliberative arenas that result from material inequality' (Cohen, 1989: 31). Second, they 'can provide the more open-ended arenas needed to form and articulate the conceptions of the common good that provide the focus of political debate in a deliberative democracy'. Cohen goes as far as to suggest that it is difficult to see how 'we can best approximate the deliberative conception . . . in the absence of strong parties, supported with public resources' (ibid.: 31–2). So, whereas, in our earlier discussion of political representatives, parties were viewed as a restricting factor on deliberations, the internal structure of parties themselves can be seen as a site that might enhance deliberation.

Aside from the role of political parties in mobilising citizens and deliberation, the model also has the advantage of direct engagement of all citizens in decision making, in terms of both casting votes and of utilising the initiative to place issues on the political agenda. Equally, deliberations among citizens and the associations of civil society would necessarily play a key role in setting the terms of debate and probably reflect the range of environmental (and non-environmental) values.

Budge stresses that such direct involvement is enabled by the 'evolution of electronically based debate and voting', thus reducing the 'extortionate time demands on ordinary citizens' typically expected within models of direct democracy (Budge, 1996: 64). Aware of the effect of economic and social inequalities on the outcomes of referendums in practice, Saward lays out in some detail the shape and scope of institutions and agencies necessary for establishing this novel form of direct democracy, including an independent 'initiative and referendum agency' to ensure some equality in agenda setting, and a 'notification and information agency' that would play a critical role in the provision of reliable information on which citizens can base their judgements. And, in direct response to the problem of material inequalities affecting participation, Saward proposes the introduction of a universal basic income scheme, a proposal that has widespread support among greens (Saward, 1998a: 104ff.).

What is clear from these brief discussions is that there are interesting possibilities available for reforming legislative assemblies. Although the idea of proxy-representation of environmental constituencies remains highly controversial (both theoretically and practically), there is certainly much scope for reform of electoral systems. More proportional systems based on multi-member constituencies and cumulative voting offer conditions conducive to increasing the representation of green parties and the diversity of perspectives and experiences of the non-human world within assemblies. Tensions may still remain between the modern practice of representation and the desire to increase the deliberative quality of debates. This may also be a problem that befalls the idea of associative democracy. However, the innovative ideas of extending the use of lot and rotation and party-based direct democracy offer imaginative possibilities that are little considered within the green or deliberative democracy literature. Combining such proposals with the ideas of constitutional environmentalists and radical, alternative visions for the green democratic polity emerge.

Civil society and the public sphere

In contemporary theories of democracy, civil society is typically understood in terms of those activities of citizens and associations that are separate and independent of either the state or the market (Keane, 1988). Given our interest in the plurality of environmental values, civil society is the location within the polity where this value pluralism will be most obviously expressed. From within green political theory, we can characterise two broad streams of thought on civil society. For those greens whose vision of the sustainable society is one of small-scale, self-sufficient political communities, the heterogeneity and moral diversity that characterises contemporary civil society undermines the development of a 'common ecological culture'. Given the ideal of small scale, such a culture is likely to be internally homogenous, insensitive to the plurality of environmental values. Rather than a separation between state and civil society, direct and unmediated relations between community members is favoured (Barry, 1999: 83ff.).

The second stream of thinking within green politics celebrates a relatively autonomous civil society as an (and for some, the most) important location for engagement. The associations of civil society offer an alternative location for the institutions of social policy. As Barry argues:

A central part of this restructuring process from a green perspective involves shifting decision-making power in regard to 'social welfare' away from the market and the state and returning it to individuals and communities. This fundamental restructuring of the definition (ends) as well as the institutions (means) of welfare is at the heart of the green aim to place the market and the state at the service of civil society rather than vice versa.

(Barry, 1999: 238)

This vision of associations as central providers of welfare has distinct resonances with the second stream of theorising on associative democracy (Hirst, 1994; 1997). Beyond the welfare provision function of voluntary associations, civil society is the home of emancipatory social movements from where challenges to political orthodoxy emerge (Dryzek, 2000a,b) and the plurality of environmental values and commitments are expressed (Torgerson, 1999).

Deliberative democratic theory particularly celebrates the contribution that institutions of civil society play in sustaining a vital public sphere orientated towards locations of power, including (but not exclusively) the state. So, for example, Seyla Benhabib argues: 'Crucial to the deliberative model of democracy is the idea of a "public sphere" of opinion-formation, debate, deliberation, and contestation among citizens, groups, movements, and organisations in a polity' (Benhabib, 1996: 80). In Jürgen Habermas's influential theory of democracy, free and spontaneous deliberation in the public sphere is fundamental to informal public opinion- and will-formation, which itself influences the formal decision-making process: 'Informal public opinion-formation generates "influence"; influence is transformed into "communicative power" through the channels of political elections; and communicative power is again transformed into "administrative power" through legislation' (Habermas, 1996b: 28; also 1996a; Squires, 2002). Habermas's emphasis on elections is rather surprising, given that it neglects the multiple channels of influence that can and do transmit public opinion, including, for example, protests, boycotts, information campaigns and the types of institutions – mediation, citizen forums, and referendums and initiatives – discussed in Chapter 4. The influence exerted on decision making by deliberations in the public sphere can take a wide variety of forms.

As we briefly discussed earlier in the book, Dryzek is concerned that critical theorists such as Habermas appear to be content with the existing institutions of liberal constitutional democracy. Dryzek argues that extra-constitutional imperatives (such as the protection of capital accumulation) limit the scope for democratic authenticity in the institutions of the state, and thus critical theorists need to concern themselves primarily with the contestation of discourses in the public sphere, particularly those discourses and movements that confront and challenge the state:

> it is important to maintain a public sphere autonomous from the state, for discursive interplay is always likely to be less constrained than within the state. It is within the public sphere that insurgent discourses and identities can first establish themselves.
>
> (Dryzek, 2000a: 79)

Dryzek argues that he offers a distinct take on deliberative democracy which he terms *discursive democracy*, a position that retains a critical orientation towards the contemporary state. The network form of organisation is particularly celebrated, with the environmental justice movement in the US being seen as a quintessential vehicle for democratic deliberation (Schlosberg, 1999; Dryzek, 2000a,b). The environmental justice movement represents an example of the cultivation of respect between diverse groups that cut across, for example, race, class and ethnicity. It is also exemplary in that it promotes 'dispersed control' over the development and framing of the environmental justice discourse (Dryzek, 2000a: 77).

Dryzek's vision of discursive democracy, with its focus on the 'progressive' and authentically democratic elements within civil society and their contribution to a vital public sphere, is important.[18] It certainly acts as a counterweight to theorists (no doubt myself included) who are optimistic about the capacity of state and state-related institutions to promote democratic deliberation. Again, his conception of discursive democracy warns against visions of governance (such as Cohen and Rogers's associative democracy and perhaps also Young's group representation) which involve high levels of direct cooperation between the state and institutions of civil society. 'Cooperation' too soon emerges as 'cooption'. However, Dryzek's position could be criticised on the grounds that it lacks a creative aspect: aside from celebrating the critical orientation of progressive networks, movements and associations towards the state, it tells us little about how we might begin to enhance deliberation in other locations. In earlier work, Dryzek hesitantly offered possible discursive designs such as mediation (Dryzek, 1990b); in more recent years, he appears to have become more sceptical about their potential.

Dryzek would probably respond by stressing the democratising impact that deliberations in the public sphere can and do have on formal decision-making processes: 'The insistently critical component of discursive democracy is well-placed to exercise vigilance over the democratic qualities of all institutions of state, legislatures and discursive designs as well as courts, and also to conduct comparative analyses of the prospects for deliberative authenticity in these institutions and the more "informal" public sphere' (Dryzek, 2000b: 86). Certainly, the types of institutions we have discussed in this book – whether restructured legislative assemblies or innovations such as mediation, citizens' forums, and referendums and initiatives – will never be able to fully reflect the plurality of environmental (and other) values within civil society. Thus, even a green state (if it were ever to emerge) would find opposition from parts of the green movement who express and prioritise alternative environmental values. A vital and pluralist civil society is an important counterweight to the activities of decision-making institutions (Torgerson, 1999).

Dryzek has argued that the activities and discourses within the public sphere do at times have profound impacts on institutional structures. 'Spontaneous order' can emerge at ecologically appropriate levels. Thus, for example, the international environmental movement has helped focus the attention of governments on the global reach of many ecological problems, leading to the development of relevant regimes. As Dryzek states: 'Defensible spontaneous orders are problem-driven and do not outlive their usefulness – unlike, for example, state bureaucracies, which are often near immortal' (Dryzek, 2000a: 160).

For green theorists, a vital civil society and public sphere is essential, in terms of both expressing the diversity of environmental values and offering opportunities for contestation and deliberation. How this plurality and deliberation is to relate to the more formal decision-making process is a matter of some debate. In this book, we have tried to envisage the possible shape of the political institutions of a more environmentally enlightened democracy. Here, institutions such as mediation, citizens forums, and referendums and initiatives are offered as potential and realistic mechanisms for the transmission of public opinion. Whatever the shape of these institutions, the public sphere is an essential element for the enhancement of democratic deliberation and the expression of the plurality of environmental values within a polity.

Conclusion

This chapter has ranged across a variety of potential institutional reforms and restructuring that could enhance democratic deliberation and the consideration of environmental values within the political process. The aim was not to offer a single blueprint for ecological democratisation, but was, rather, more speculative in scope. Inevitably, institutional design involves difficult judgements about the relevant context – whether political, social, economic or environmental – and the potential trade-offs that may be necessary between institutional goods such as deliberation, representation and efficiency. There is no single institutional model that will be ideal in all circumstances. Actually existing liberal democracies have different constitutional and legislative arrangements, variations in the institutions of civil society and divergent traditions in the use of mechanisms such as mediation, citizen forums, referendums and initiatives. Proposals for reform and restructuring need to account for these differences. What is required is imagination and sensitivity to context in crafting potential changes, and a willingness to experiment and learn lessons from both success and, perhaps more importantly, failure.

Concluding remarks

In this book I have offered three broad responses to the question of how political institutions can be structured so that they are sensitive to environmental values. My first point is that we need to recognise that there is a plurality of environmental values which are often incompatible and incommensurable. It is therefore important to create political institutions that promote reflection on and consideration of the wide range of environmental values that citizens hold.

My second argument is based on a critique of existing political institutions. Widely favoured appraisal techniques, such as cost–benefit analysis, often fail to incorporate the whole range of environmental values and fail to reflect the way in which we commonly make judgements about non-human nature.

My final argument develops constructive suggestions as to how political institutions might be restructured to allow greater democratic deliberation. It is my belief that such a move would foster decision making that is more sensitive to environmental values and considerations. Deliberative institutions cannot *guarantee* green outcomes or even the prioritisation of environmental values, but they can provide a conducive context within which the variety of environmental values can be voiced and considered in decision-making processes. Political judgements and decisions that truly reflect the plurality of environmental values might then begin to emerge.

The aim of this book has not been to promote a definitive blueprint of the 'green democratic polity'. Rather, it can be seen as a contribution to the imaginative and practical task of rethinking democratic institutions so that they are sensitive to the plurality of environmental values. This is a difficult undertaking but nonetheless an urgent one.

This book can thus be read as an appeal to both democratic and green theorists to consider more carefully the question of institutional design. Both democratic and green political thought have been relatively successful in arguing the case for institutional change. The task now is to realise the institutional implications of these theoretical and conceptual ideas.

Notes

1 Value pluralism and the environment

1 The deep ecology platform has appeared in slightly different formats in different publications. For a sustained analysis of the work of Arne Naess, see Witoszek and Brennan (1999).

2 The critique of intrinsic value theories draws on a range of sources, including Stone (1988), Thompson (1990), O'Neill (1993), T. Hayward (1995; 1998) and Soper (1995).

3 The analysis of intrinsic value theories offered here is rather cursory and is not intended to detail the different strategies taken by environmental philosophers. There are important differences between theorists who follow a strategy of (1) moral extensionism (either broadly utilitarian or neo-Kantian), isolating a feature of human existence that is viewed as morally considerable and then demonstrating that certain non-human entities also display the requisite feature; and (2) isolating a specific feature of the natural world which then 'trumps' other types of value that humans may recognise and wish to promote.

4 This point is developed in more detail in Thompson (1990: 147–60) and T. Hayward (1995: 62–72; 1998: 42–58).

5 See, for example, Hepburn (1984), O'Neill (1993) and Williams (1995).

6 The examples that follow draw on Hepburn's work, and also on John Benson's useful categorisation of his ideas (Benson, 2000: 72).

7 Similarly, Hayward highlights practices such as hunting species to extinction and the destruction of precious environments for road building and industrial development to make the point that charges of 'anthropocentrism' fail to illuminate the fact that such practices do not necessarily serve 'human interests in general, but the interests of one quite narrowly-defined group . . . it is unhelpful to cover over this fundamental point and criticise humanity in general for practices carried out by a limited number of humans when many others may in fact oppose it . . . not only unhelpful, but positively counterproductive. It is not only conceptually

mistaken, but also a practical and strategic mistake, to criticise humanity in general for practices of specific groups of humans' (Hayward, 1997: 57–8).

8 A number of writers have analysed the importance of virtues in green politics. See, for example, Hill (1994), Barry (1999), O'Neill (1993) and Cooper (1995).

9 R. M. Hare is particularly critical of the use of contrived and hypothetical examples in moral philosophy (Hare, 1981: 47–51).

10 The account of value pluralism offered here draws on a variety of sources from within mainstream moral philosophy, including Bernard Williams (1981; 1985), John Gray (1995; 2000), Joseph Raz (1986), John Kekes (1993), Stuart Hampshire (1983; 1989) and Thomas Nagel (1979a), and from pluralists within environmental ethics such as Christopher Stone (1987; 1988) and Andrew Brennan (1992).

11 When faced with conflicting values, O'Neill argues that only weak comparisons may be possible: it may simply be the case that the values cannot be either cardinally or ordinally ranked (O'Neill, 1993: 103–6).

12 Raz contends that, when faced with incompatible and incommensurable alternatives, 'we are in a sense free to choose which course to follow. That sense of freedom is special, and may be misleading . . . . Incomparability . . . does not mean indifference. It marks the inability of reason to guide our action, not the insignificance of our choice' (Raz 1986: 334).

13 A number of moral theorists have investigated this sense of loss, including Williams (1973a: 166–86), Sen (1987: 67), Wolf (1992: 788) and Kekes (1993: 11).

14 The form of perspectivism offered here is misrepresented if it is understood simply as moral (and epistemological) relativism with 'no criteria for saying that one perspective is better than any other perspective' (Owen 1995: 33). Following David Owen, there appears to be some confusion between the claim that all perspectives have an equal right to claim moral or epistemic authority (perspectivism) and the claim that we grant them equal authority (relativism). Perspectivism recognises that there are contextual standards of rationality associated with the values we appeal to in ethical reasoning that allow us to distinguish between the different claims to ethical authority (ibid.: 33–4). Of course, we may still be left with ethical conflicts.

15 Along similar lines, Friedrich Nietzsche argues: 'There is only a perspectivist seeing, only a perspectivist "knowing": the more affects we allow to speak about a thing, the more eyes we are able to use for the same thing, the more complete will be our "concept" of the thing, our "objectivity"' (Nietzsche 1994: 92).

2 Environmental economics and the internalisation of environmental values

1 See, in particular, the work of the National Center for Environmental Economics within the EPA: www.epa.gov/economics.

2 It is the work of environmental economists working within the liberal, neo-classical framework that is the subject of this chapter and this should not be conflated with either institutional economics (e.g. Jacobs, 1994) or ecological economics (e.g. Georgescu-Roegen, 1971).

3 This book has proved so popular and influential that Pearce and his colleagues published a series of *Blueprint* texts on different aspects of economic valuation of environmental issues, from global environmental change to the cost of transport.

4 Rather confusingly, policy guidance was published in 1998 with the same title, *Policy Appraisal and the Environment*. This was a much less rigorous document, and the original and more detailed 1991 publication is still referenced within this new guidance. Until recently, the 1998 guidance was available on the Internet, but it appears to have vanished into the ether during the change from the Department of Environment, Transport and the Regions (DETR) to the Department of Environment, Food and Rural Affairs (DEFRA) in 2001.

5 For the full text of 'The Green Book', see www.hm-treasury.gov.uk/mediastore/otherfiles/96.pdf.

6 This perhaps explains why some departments have been hostile to the introduction of extended CBA.

7 Pareto optimality, with its focus on changes in individuals' utility functions, can be seen as one of the surviving utilitarian criteria within modern economics. The onslaught of positivism within the discipline saw the discrediting of interpersonal comparisons of utility, both on scientific and ethical grounds, and it seems to be the case that the survival of Pareto optimality as a decision-making criterion has as much to do with its practical usage as with its theoretical standing (Sen, 1987: 30ff.; Pearce and Nash, 1981: 2–4). Under the influence of positivism, many practitioners of CBA argue that Pareto optimality is 'value free' and makes no normative claims. This will be shown to be a vacuous assertion.

8 For a more detailed discussion of techniques and some of the problems associated with them, see OECD (1989: 25–58), Pearce and Turner (1990: 141–59) and Winpenny (1991: 42–72).

9 See, for example, the numerous articles in the *Journal of Environmental Economics and Management* devoted to the results and refinement of CVM. For a discussion among economists of methodological issues raised by CVM, see Bjornstad and Kahn (1996).

10 This discussion of biases draws on the work of, for example, Pearce and Turner (1990: 149–53), Jacobs (1991: 205ff.) and Winpenny (1991: 59–61).

11 For a systematic defence of the use of utilitarianism as a guiding philosophy in government decision making, see Goodin (1995: 60ff.).

12 It is not within the remit of this book to question the use of such a model generally within economic theory. It appears that *homo economicus*, the rational, self-interested individual, may be a powerful and useful idealisation in modelling consumer behaviour in very specific market situations. However, what is to be addressed in this chapter is the extent to which such a heuristic model can serve as the basis for judgements when moving into the field of policy analysis and political decision making.

13 Cass Sunstein contends that taking market behaviour as a guide to preferences is highly problematic as people will adapt themselves 'to undue limitations in current practices and opportunities' (Sunstein, 1991: 21). He argues that poverty 'is perhaps the most severe obstacle to the free development of preferences and beliefs' (ibid.: 23).

14 Pearce and C. A. Nash recognise that a 'distributional judgement is made whether the analyst wishes to make it or not' (Pearce and Nash, 1981: 20). Thus, individual preferences 'should be weighted by some "intensity" factor which will be correlated with the individual's income' (ibid: 10). But what should the 'intensity' factor be and what if, because of information or social or economic constraints, the individual does not express certain preferences in the first place? An alternative approach is taken by John Harsanyi, who argues that analysts should focus on 'true' rather than 'manifest' preferences: 'a person's true preferences are the preferences he *would* have if he had all the relevant factual information, always reasoned with the greatest possible care, and were in a state of mind most conducive to rational choice' (Harsanyi, 1982: 55). But who is to elucidate such 'true' preferences?

15 Even Wilfred Beckerman, a frequent and vociferous critic of environmentalists, has accepted that it is a mistake to treat environmental values in the same way as commodities, and that the way we value the non-human world cannot be adequately expressed in economic terms (Beckerman and Pasek, 1997: 73–5).

16 The substitutability debate in environmental economics centres around whether all forms of capital are substitutable (weak sustainability) or whether natural and human/human-made capital should be seen as complementary (strong sustainability). The recognition by many environmental economists that sustainability constraints are required in the use of CBA to ensure that 'critical natural capital' is preserved exposes the limits to the substitutability thesis, even when thinking of the environment as a resource. See, for example, Pearce *et al.* (1989: 34ff.), the discussion on natural capital by Holland (1994), the exchange between Beckerman (1995), Daly (1995) and Jacobs (1995), and Dobson (1998).

17 For more on the environmental critique of economic valuation, see Jacobs (1994; 1997), Knetsch (1994), Vadnjal and O'Connor (1994), and Keat (1997).

18 Robert Sugden and Alan Williams argue that such problems are avoided simply by assessing only the costs and benefits that are of importance to the decision maker (Sugden and Williams, 1978: 232–41).

19 The Department of Transport (DOT) was merged into the Department of the Environment, Transport and the Regions (DETR) under the incoming Labour administration in 1997. After the 2001 general election, the Department of Transport, Local Government and the Regions (DTLR) was established. A year later, a free-standing Department for Transport (DfT) once more emerged.

20 To be fair to Pearce, he is aware of the problem of equity and he argues for the use of 'sensitivity analysis', which allows CBAs to 'identify the incidence of costs and benefits on different groups' (Pearce, 1998: 94; also HM Treasury, 1997: 20). However, this proposal still suffers from the problem that individuals need to have expressed preferences for them to be included within any analysis. As argued above, contextual factors may inhibit such expression.

21 For a critical analysis of ecological modernisation, see Hajer (1995), Christoff (1996a), Gouldson and Murphy (1997) and Connelly and Smith (2003).

22 Aldo Leopold's land ethic holds that 'A thing is right when it tends to preserve the integrity, stability and beauty of the biotic community. It is wrong when it does otherwise' (Leopold, in Dobson, 1991: 240–1). The principle of biospherical egalitarianism is the second strand of Naess' original exposition of the ideas of the deep ecology movement (Naess, 1973: 95–100).

23 The Department for Transport (established in 2002 – see footnote 19) now uses an innovative multi-modal approach for the appraisal of transport proposals. However, COBA is still used for the evaluation of individual road schemes. The values of time savings and accidents have been updated to take into account inflation and new research, but the controversial principles remain the same. For further information, see www.dft.gov.uk. For a sustained argument that COBA should be extended to include environmental valuations, see Bateman *et al.* (1993).

24 COBA does include at least one environmental cost of road construction: the price of land. The incorporation of market prices for certain types of land is controversial because it may result in an acute underestimate. Green belt land, Sites of Special Scientific Interest (SSSIs) and Areas of Outstanding Natural Beauty (AONBs) are protected areas, ones which have severe development restrictions attached to them because of their ecological value. However, when a decision is made to propose a road scheme through such environments, the value of the land is then incorporated. But one of the primary features of such areas is that they have planning restrictions attached to them, and so the market price is extremely low, a price that clearly misrepresents the important scientific, aesthetic or amenity value of the land in question. Not only is an area of

local or national importance to be lost, but its value is taken to be *less* than that of ordinary agricultural land. The DOT's own standing advisory committee recognised this paradox: 'the cost of acquired land . . . may be a serious underestimate of its social value if the land is subject to severe restrictions on development' (Standing Advisory Committee on Trunk Road Assessment – SACTRA, 1992: 96). English Nature estimated that the DOT's 1989 *Roads for Prosperity* road programme threatened 161 SSSIs, and English Heritage calculated that over 800 important archaeological sites could be affected.

3 Deliberative democracy and green political theory

1 Deliberative democracy has also been termed discursive (Dryzek, 2000a,b) and communicative (Young, 1996) democracy. Although these terms are used interchangeably by many authors, elements of the distinct positions of John Dryzek and Iris Marion Young will be discussed in the following chapters. For a useful typology of theories of deliberative democracy, see Blaug (1996).

2 As we shall discuss in the next chapter, the recognition that a division of political labour is necessary separates deliberative democracy from some conceptions of direct and participative democracy popular within green politics.

3 It is for this reason that Benjamin Barber criticises procedural liberalism, which he argues is 'at best a politics of static interests, never a politics of transformation' (Barber, 1984: 24).

4 Benhabib terms these conditions the principle of universal moral respect and the principle of egalitarian reciprocity (Benhabib, 1992: 29).

5 Strategic or instrumental rationality is a means–end form of reasoning: 'the capacity to devise, select, and effect good means to clarified ends'. It may be unavoidable in the implementation of decisions, but, with respect to political argumentation and dialogue, it 'destroys the more congenial, spontaneous, egalitarian and intrinsically meaningful aspects of human association' (Dryzek, 1990b: 4). Jürgen Habermas captures the concept of an understanding-oriented deliberative or 'communicative' action by setting it against strategic action. Both types of action are social action characterised by meanings 'as intended by the actor or actors' which are 'orientated' in that they take 'account of the behaviour of others'. The orientation of strategic action is towards success, that is 'the appearance in the world of a desired state, which can in a given situation, be causally produced through goal-oriented action or omission'. As such, strategic action follows the rules of rational choice, and impacts on the decisions of rational 'opponents'. Habermas argues that competent speakers can themselves tell when they strategically attempt to influence causally a hearer's action, when they use means such as deceit, manipulation and coercion to bring about compliance. Communicative action, in contrast, is

defined by actors oriented 'not through egocentric calculations of success but through acts aiming towards reaching understanding' (Habermas, 1981: 279–86).

6 The target of such criticisms is the work of Habermas, in particular his insistence that the only force that should operate in political decision making is 'that of the better argument' (Habermas, 1975: 108).

7 This broader conception of deliberation is central to Young's conception of 'communicative democracy'. As we shall see, this also includes a sceptical orientation towards the ideal of consensus. Young's argument about the role of storytelling and narrative in broadening mutual understanding within democratic dialogue resembles Lynn Sanders' notion of testimony (Sanders, 1997). For a critique of these arguments see Miller (2002).

8 Thus the 'ideal speech situation' becomes a powerful standard against which to judge moral and political arrangements.

9 Amy Gutmann and Dennis Thompson further elaborate these 'principles of accommodation' that underlie mutual respect in *Democracy and Disagreement* (1996). Their account of deliberative democracy also includes 'principles of preclusion' (Gutmann and Thompson, 1996: 76–9). However, the form in which these are expressed is based on a particularly strict account of morality that limits the possible issues that can be deliberated upon. In a similar manner to John Rawls (1993), Gutmann and Thompson have limited what is to be judged as suitable for political debate such that the openness of deliberation is compromised.

10 See, for example, Dryzek (1987; 1995; 2000a), Dobson (1996b), Goodin (1996), Hayward (1998), Barry (1999), Eckersley (1999; 2000) and Torgerson (1999).

11 Such pragmatic epistemological arguments differ from a *strong* epistemological defence of deliberative democracy in which legitimacy is identified with the correctness of the outcome of deliberation (Estlund, 1997).

12 However, Dryzek's generalisable interest in 'the human life-support capacity of natural systems' (Dryzek, 1987: 204) is a precondition not just of deliberative democracy, but of all political arrangements. As Andrew Dobson argues, 'while we might agree that a functioning ecosystem is a precondition for human communication, it is radically indeterminate – it seems – as regards types of communication' (Dobson, 1996b: 139). As an action-guiding norm, it tells us next to nothing about the level and nature of intervention, beyond a presumption against the complete destruction of the human life-support system.

13 Bronwyn Hayward appears to make a similar point with respect to the different elements of communication used by New Zealand's Maori communities to express their relationship with the natural world (B. Hayward, 1995: 225).

14 Marcel Wissenburg is not at all convinced by the claim that deliberative democracy will improve the moral quality of decision making in the way

that Goodin and other green proponents contend (Wissenburg, 1998: 222–4).

15 Gundersen's research is based on one-to-one interviews. In line with the theoretical arguments, the deliberative process allowed Gundersen's interviewees to follow through the implications of and, in many cases, to challenge their own existing values, beliefs and interests. Although offering some interesting evidence, the intimacy and supportiveness of one-to-one discussions do not adequately reflect the potential anxieties and fears inherent in full-scale political dialogue.

16 Confusingly, Habermas's *moral* theory is termed discourse *ethics* (Habermas, 1990; 1993). His work on discourse ethics differs in important respects from his earlier work on quasi-transcendental interests (Habermas, 1971).

17 These are the two works that have been translated into English in which he has discussed the controversies about the status of non-human nature in some depth.

18 We will have more to say about the idea of agency in nature below.

19 This is an example of how the deliberative account offered in this chapter differs from the position of Gutmann and Thompson (1990; 1996) and Rawls (1993), who wish to preclude certain claims prior to political dialogue.

20 One of the ways in which Dryzek derives agency in nature is from the Gaia hypothesis (Dryzek, 1990a: 205; 2000a: 150). Similar sympathetic arguments for the extension of the principle of agency and/or autonomy into aspects of the non-human world are offered by Eckersley (1995: 181–94; 1999) and Dobson (1996b: 142–4).

21 For examples of such comparisons, see Benhabib (1992), D'Entreves (2002), Miller (1992) and Habermas (1996a).

4 Three deliberative models

1 Thus, one of the problems of CBA – isolating the relevant constituency (see Chapter 2) – is also a problem in establishing deliberative institutions.

2 These potential locations of democratic dialogue will be discussed in more detail in Chapter 5.

3 Renn *et al.* (1995) offer a complementary evaluation of various forms of citizen participation, including mediation and citizens' juries, using 'Habermasian' criteria of fairness and competence.

4 More than one thousand non-governmental organisations are accredited to participate in the Commission's work.

5 The UK Sustainable Development Commission subsumed the work of the UK Roundtable on Sustainable Development and the British Government Panel on Sustainable Development. See www.sd-commission.gov.uk.

6 The term 'citizen forum' will be used as there is no recognised term that embraces this type of institutional innovation (Smith, 2000).

7 In Germany, a number of juries have been run concurrently and/or in series. To date, the largest project involved 500 citizens from all over Germany.

8 In the UK, the Institute for Public Policy Research (IPPR), the King's Fund Policy Institute and the Local Government Management Board (LGMB) promoted and sponsored a series of citizens' juries in the mid- and late 1990s. These were typically conducted in conjunction with local government or health authorities, two institutions often criticised for failing to engage their local populations (Coote and Lenaghan, 1997; Coote and Mattinson, 1997; Hall and Stewart, 1997; McIver, 1997).

9 For information on the second UKNCC, see http://www.ukceed.org/.

10 Dienel faces a similar problem of collating results when he runs a series of juries on the same issue.

11 Saward meticulously sets out the shape and scope of institutions and agencies necessary to establish a fair and equal form of direct democracy through initiatives and referendums (Saward, 1998a: 104ff.).

5 Towards ecological democratisation

1 This phrase is borrowed from Hayward (2000).

2 We have already discussed Dryzek's arguments about ecological preconditions in relation to democratic deliberation in Chapter 3.

3 Saward's concerns resonate with the demands of the environmental justice movement in the US (Schlosberg, 1999).

4 The most widely supported non-human animals for inclusion within constitutional rights are the great apes (Cavalieri and Singer, 1993).

5 In her defence, Eckersley cites the existence of 'class actions' and the existence of legal entities such as corporations and the state (Eckersley, 1995: 189).

6 The full text of the Aarhus Convention can be found at www.unece.org.

7 Eckersley argues for the phrase 'to present and future human generations and non-human communities' to be added to the Rio Declaration's precautionary principle. This 'would head off narrow, anthropocentric interpretations of this decision rule' (Eckersley, 2000: 130). See O'Riordan and Jordan (1995) for a discussion of competing interpretations of the principle.

8 Constitutional environmentalism is thus best understood in the same way that deliberative democratic theory understands the role of the constitution. For example, Benhabib argues that the basic rights and liberties that make up a constitution should be 'viewed as rules of the game that can be contested within the game but only insofar as one first accepts to abide by them and play the game at all' (Benhabib, 1996: 80).

9 The analysis that follows primarily focuses on the role of representative assemblies. It does not consider the role and structure of the executive: arguments for altering the relative significance of ministries so that the

environment ministry clears spending and other proposals from across government (Saward, 1998b: 352), and other ways that the machinery of government can be restructured to integrate environmental considerations across all policy areas, will not be discussed.

10 Only in rare situations do a voter's values, commitments and preferences coincide with those of a candidate: this is the paradigm case for concentrating votes on a single candidate. Given the agglomeration of issues in party platforms, it is more likely that there is a weaker relationship between the perspectives of voter and candidates.

11 Eckersley has argued that the democratic turn in green political theory is part of a wider cultural and political emancipatory project that is responding to the contemporary 'cultural malaise and the need for cultural renewal': 'This is reflected in the concern of emancipatory theorists to find ways of theoretically integrating the concerns of the ecology movement with other new social movements, particularly those concerned with feminism, peace and Third World aid and development. This new theoretical project is concerned to find ways of overcoming the destructive logic of capital accumulation, the acquisitive values of consumer society, and, more generally, all systems of domination (including class domination, patriarchy, imperialism, racism, totalitarianism, and the domination of nature)' (Eckersley, 1992: 20–1).

12 *Self*-organisation and *self*-empowerment are important characteristics in order to overcome charges of essentialism in group representation.

13 The representation of non-nationals is taken to be best secured through either transnational parliaments or other intergovernmental institutions (Dobson, 1996b: 131).

14 Kavka and Warren's strategy will not be discussed here. Their suggested mechanisms not only include a direct election of representatives (similar to Mills), but also the presidential appointment of an 'environmental guardian' or the creation of a ministry or agency charged with protecting the interests of the environmental constituency. These last two suggestions refer specifically to the structure of the executive rather than the legislative assembly.

15 We can agree with Dobson that if such a hierarchy of moral worth is to be constructed it should not be left to philosophers or scientists, but rather 'constructed discursively by the proxy constituency' (Dobson, 1996b: 138).

16 Elster offers a complementary analysis of constitution making using four criteria: size, publicity, force and interest (Elster, 1998).

17 However, while removing one part of the political class (political representatives) another element – the civil service – remains untouched and may well gain power, given the political inexperience of citizens.

18 Dryzek (unlike some other theorists) is well aware that the contestation of discourses within the public sphere does not necessarily signify discursive

democracy (Dryzek, 2000a: 76; 2000b: 87). The activities of many groups within civil society and the pervasive influence of the state and the market economy frequently undermine the democratic nature of deliberations in the public sphere.

References

Abramson, J. (1994) *We, The Jury*, New York: Basic Books.

Achterberg, W. (1996a) 'Sustainability, Community and Democracy', in Doherty, B. and de Geus, M. (eds), *Democracy and Green Political Thought*, London: Routledge.

Achterberg, W. (1996b) 'Sustainability and Associative Democracy', in Lafferty, W. M. and Meadowcroft, J. (eds), *Democracy and the Environment*, Cheltenham: Edward Elgar.

Adams, J. (1995) *Cost Benefit Analysis: Part of the Problem, Not the Solution*, Oxford: Green College Centre for Environmental Policy and Understanding.

Aldred, J. and Jacobs, M. (1997) *Citizens and Wetlands: Report of the Ely Citizens' Jury*, Lancaster: Centre for the Study of Environmental Change.

Amy, D. (1987) *The Politics of Mediation*, New York: Columbia University Press.

Arblaster, A. (1987) *Democracy*, Buckingham: Open University Press.

Arendt, H. (1968) *Between Past and Future*, New York: Viking Press.

Arendt, H. (1982) *Lectures on Kant's Political Philosophy*, Chicago: University of Chicago Press.

Atkins, S.T. (1990) *Unspoken Decrees: Road Appraisal, Democracy and the Environment*, London: South East Wildlife Trust.

Attfield, R. (1991) *The Ethics of Environmental Concern*, 2nd edn, Athens, GA: University of Georgia Press.

Barber, B. (1984) *Strong Democracy: Participatory Politics for a New Age*, Berkeley, CA: California University Press.

Barde, J. and Pearce, D. (1991) *Valuing the Environment*, London: Earthscan.

Barry, J. (1999) *Rethinking Green Politics*, London: Sage.

Bateman, I., Turner, R.K. and Bateman, S. (1993) 'Extending Cost Benefit Analysis of UK Highway Proposals: Environmental Evaluation and Equity', *Project Appraisal*, 8, 4: 213–24.

Baughman, M. (1995) 'Mediation', in Renn, O., Webler, T. and Wiedermann, P. (eds), *Fairness and Competence in Citizen Participation*, Dordrecht: Kluwer.

Baynes, K. (1995) 'Democracy and the *Rechtsstaat*: Habermas's *Faktizitat und Geltung*', in White, S. (ed.), *The Cambridge Companion to Habermas*, Cambridge: Cambridge University Press.

Beck, U. (1992) *Risk Society*, London: Sage.

Beckerman, W. (1995) 'How Would You Like Your "Sustainability", Sir? Weak or Strong? A Reply to my Critics', *Environmental Values*, 4: 169–79.

Beckerman, W. and Pasek, J. (1997) 'Plural Values and Environmental Valuation', *Environmental Values*, 6, 1: 65–86.

Beetham, D. (1992) 'Liberal Democracy and the Limits of Democratisation', *Prospects for Democracy: Political Studies Special Issue*, 40: 40–53.

Benhabib, S. (1992) *Situating the Self*, Cambridge: Polity.

Benhabib, S. (1996) 'Toward a Deliberative Model of Democratic Legitimacy', in Benhabib, S. (ed.), *Democracy and Difference*, Princeton, NJ: Princeton University Press.

Benson, J. (2000) *Environmental Ethics: An Introduction with Readings*, London: Routledge.

Bentley, R. and Owen, D. (2001) 'Ethical Loyalties, Civic Virtue and the Circumstances of Politics', *Philosophical Explorations*, 9, 3: 223–38.

Benton, T. (1993) *Ecology, Animal Rights and Social Justice*, London: Verso.

Bjornstad, D. and Kahn, J. (eds) (1996) *The Contingent Valuation of Environmental Resources*, Cheltenham: Edward Elgar.

Blackburn, J.W. and Bruce, W.M. (eds) (1995) *Mediating Environmental Conflicts: Theory and Practice*, Westport, CT: Quorum.

Blaug, R. (1996) 'New Theories of Discursive Democracy: A User's Guide', *Philosophy and Social Criticism*, 22, 1: 49–80.

Bohman, J. (1998) 'The Coming of Age of Deliberative Democracy', *The Journal of Political Philosophy*, 6, 4: 400–25.

Bookchin, M. (1987) 'Social Ecology versus 'Deep Ecology': A Challenge for the Ecology Movement, *Green Perspectives*, 4/5.

Bookchin, M. (1991) *The Ecology of Freedom*, 2nd edn, Montreal: Black Rose.

Bowler, S. and Donovan, T. (2001) 'Popular Control of Referendum Agendas: Implications for Democratic Outcomes and Minority Rights', in Mendleson, M. and Parkin, A. (eds), *Referendum Democracy: Citizens, Elites and Deliberation in Referendum Campaigns*, Basingstoke: Palgrave.

Bray, J. (1995) *Spend, Spend, Spend: How the Department of Transport Wastes Money and Mismanages the Roads Programme*, London: Transport 2000.

Brennan, A. (1992) 'Moral Pluralism and the Environment', *Environmental Values*, 1, 1: 15–33.

Budge, I. (1996) *The New Challenge of Direct Democracy*, Cambridge: Polity.

Budge, I. (2001) 'Political Parties in Direct Democracy', in Mendleson, M. and Parkin, A. (eds), *Referendum Democracy: Citizens, Elites and Deliberation in Referendum Campaigns*, Basingstoke: Palgrave.

Burnheim, J. (1985) *Is Democracy Possible?*, Cambridge: Polity.

Callicott, J. B. (1990) 'The Case Against Moral Pluralism', *Environmental Ethics*, 12, 3: 100–24.

Callicott, J. B. (1995) 'Animal Liberation: A Triangular Affair', in Elliot, R. (ed.), *Environmental Ethics*, Oxford: Oxford University Press.

Cavalieri, P. and Singer, P. (1993) *The Great Ape Project: Equality Beyond Humanity*, London: Fourth Estate.

Center for Deliberative Polling (2001) *Deliberative Polling Blue Book*, www.la.utexas.edu/research/delpol/bluebook/summary.html.

Chambers, S. (1995) 'Discourse and Democratic Practices', in White, S. (ed.), *The Cambridge Companion to Habermas*, Cambridge: Cambridge University Press.

Chambers, S. (2001) 'Constitutional Referendums and Democratic Deliberation', in Mendleson, M. and Parkin, A. (eds), *Referendum Democracy: Citizens, Elites and Deliberation in Referendum Campaigns*, Basingstoke: Palgrave.

Christoff, P. (1996a) 'Ecological Modernisation, Ecological Modernities', *Environmental Politics*, 5, 3: 476–500.

Christoff, P. (1996b) 'Ecological Citizens and Ecologically Guided Democracy', in Doherty, B. and De Geus, M. (eds), *Democracy and Green Political Thought*, London: Routledge.

Cohen, J. (1989) 'Deliberation and Democratic Legitimacy', in Hamlin, A. and Pettit, P. (eds), *The Good Polity: Normative Analysis of the State*, Oxford: Oxford University Press.

Cohen, J. (1996) 'Procedure and Substance in Deliberative Democracy', in Benhabib, S. (ed.), *Democracy and Difference*, Princeton, NJ: Princeton University Press.

Cohen, J. and Rogers, J. (1995) 'Secondary Associations and Democratic Governance', in Wright, E. O. (ed.), *Associations and Democracy*, London: Verso.

Connelly, J. and Smith, G. (2003) *Politics and the Environment: From Theory to Practice*, 2nd edn, London: Routledge.

Cooper, D. (1995) 'Other Species and Moral Reason', in Cooper, D. and Palmer, J. (eds), *Just Environments: Intergenerational, International and Interspecies*, London: Routledge.

Coote, A. and Lenaghan, J. (1997) *Citizens' Juries: Theory into Practice*, London: IPPR.

Coote, A. and Mattinson, D. (1997) *Twelve Good Neighbours*, London: Fabian Society.

Copp, D. (1985) 'Morality, Reason, and Management Science: the Rationale of Cost–benefit analysis', in Paul, E.F., Miller, F.D. and Paul, J. (eds), *Ethics and Economics*, Oxford: Blackwell.

Cronin, T.E. (1989) *Direct Democracy: The Politics of Initiative, Referendum and Recall*, Cambridge, MA: Harvard University Press.

Crosby, N. (1995) 'Citizen Juries: One Solution for Difficult Environmental Questions', in Renn, O., Webler, T. and Wiedermann, P. (eds), *Fairness and Competence in Citizen Participation*, Dordrecht: Kluwer.

D'Agostino, F. (1990) 'Ethical Pluralism and the Role of Opposition in Democratic Politics', *The Monist*, 73, 3: 437–63.

Dalvi, M. (1988) *The Value of Life and Safety: A Search for a Consensus Estimate*, London: Department of Transport.

Daly, H. (1995) 'On Wilfred Beckerman's Critique of Sustainable Development', *Environmental Values*, 4: 49–55.

D'Entreves, M.P. (2002) 'Political Legitimacy and Democratic Deliberation', in D'Entreves, M. P. (ed.), *Democracy as Public Deliberation*, Manchester: Manchester University Press.

Department of the Environment (DOE) (1991) *Policy Appraisal and the Environment: A guide for Government Departments*, London: HMSO.

Department of Environment, Food and Rural Affairs (DEFRA) (2002) *Achieving a Better Quality of Life: Review of Progress Towards Sustainable Development: Government Annual Report 2001*, London: DEFRA.

Department of Transport (DOT) (1987) *Values for Journey Time Savings and Accident Prevention*: London: DOT.

DOT (1989), *Roads for Prosperity*, London: HMSO.

DOT (1991), *The Role of Investment Appraisal in Road and Rail Transport*, London: HMSO.

DOT (1992) *The Government's Expenditure Plans For Transport 1992–93 to 1994–5*, London: HMSO.

Devall, B. and Sessions, G. (1985) *Deep Ecology: Living as if Nature Mattered*, Salt Lake City, UT: Peregrine and Smith.

Dienel, P. (1996) 'Das "Burgergutachten" und seine Nebenwirkungen' (translated by Corrine Wales as 'The "Citizens Report" and its Wider Effects'), *Forum fur Interdisziplinare Forschung*, 17: 113–35.

Dienel, P. and Renn, O. (1995) 'Planning Cells: A Gate to "Fractal" Mediation', in Renn, O., Webler, T. and Wiedermann, P. (eds), *Fairness and Competence in Citizen Participation*, Dordrecht: Kluwer.

Dobson, A. (ed.) (1990) *The Green Reader*, London: André Deutsch.

Dobson, A. (1993) 'Critical Theory and Green Politics', in Dobson, A. and Lucardie, P. (eds), *The Politics of Nature: Explorations in Green Political Theory*, London: Routledge.

Dobson, A. (1996a) 'Democratising Green Theory: Preconditions and Principles', in Doherty, B. and de Geus, M. (eds), *Democracy and Green Political Thought*, London: Routledge.

Dobson, A. (1996b) 'Representative Democracy and the Environment', in Lafferty, W. and Meadowcroft, J. (eds), *Democracy and the Environment: Problems and Prospects*, Cheltenham: Edward Elgar.

Dobson, A. (1998) *Justice and the Environment*, Oxford: Oxford University Press.

Dryzek, J.S. (1987) *Rational Ecology: Environment and Political Economy*, Oxford: Blackwell.

Dryzek, J.S. (1990a) 'Green Reason: Communicative Ethics and the Biosphere', *Environmental Ethics*, 12: 195–210.

Dryzek, J.S. (1990b) *Discursive Democracy: Politics, Policy, and Political Science*, Cambridge: Cambridge University Press.

Dryzek, J.S. (1995) 'Political and Ecological Communication', *Environmental Politics*, 4, 4: 13–30.

Dryzek, J.S. (2000a) *Deliberative Democracy and Beyond: Liberals, Critics, Contestations*, Oxford: Oxford University Press.

Dryzek, J.S. (2000b) 'Discursive democracy vs. liberal constitutionalism', in Saward, M. (ed.), *Democratic Innovation: Deliberation, Representation and Association*, London: Routledge.

Dukes, E.F. (1996) *Resolving Public Conflict*. Manchester: Manchester University Press.

Eckersley, R. (1992) *Environmentalism and Political Theory*, London: UCL Press.

Eckersley, R. (1995) 'Liberal Democracy and the Rights of Nature: The Struggle for Inclusion', *Environmental Politics*, 4, 4: 169–98.

Eckersley, R. (1996) 'Greening Liberal Democracy: The Rights Discourse Revisited', in Doherty, B. and de Geus, M. (eds), *Democracy and Green Political Thought*, London: Routledge.

Eckersley, R. (1999) 'The Discourse Ethic and the Problem of Representing Nature', *Environmental Politics*, 8, 2: 24–49.

Eckersley, R. (2000) 'Deliberative Democracy, Ecological Representation and Risk: Towards a Democracy of the Affected', in Saward, M. (ed.), *Democratic Innovation: Deliberation, Representation and Association*, London: Routledge.

The Ecologist (1993) *Whose Common Future?*, London: Earthscan.

Elliot, R. (1995) 'Faking Nature', in Elliot, R. (ed.), *Environmental Ethics*, Oxford: Oxford University Press.

Ellison, C. (1991) 'Dispute Resolution and Democratic Theory', in Nagel, S. and Mills, M. (eds), *Systematic Analysis in Dispute Resolution*, New York: Quorum.

Elster, J. (1998) 'Deliberation and Constitution Making', in Elster, J. (ed.), *Deliberative Democracy*, Cambridge: Cambridge University Press.

Eriksen, E.O. (2000) 'The European Union's Democratic Deficit: A Deliberative Perspective', in Saward, M. (ed.), *Democratic Innovation: Deliberation, Representation and Association*, London: Routledge.

Estlund, D. (1997) 'Beyond Fairness and Deliberation: The Epistemic Dimension of Democratic Authority', in Bohman, J.F. and Rehg, W. (eds), *Deliberative Democracy*, Cambridge, MA: MIT Press.

Fearon, J.D. (1998) 'Deliberation as Discussion', in Elster, J. (ed.), *Deliberative Democracy*, Cambridge: Cambridge University Press.

Fiorino, D. (1995) 'Regulatory Negotiation as a Form of Public Participation', in Renn, O., Webler, T. and Wiedermann, P. (eds), *Fairness and Competence in Citizen Participation*, Dordrecht: Kluwer.

Fischer, F. (2000) *Citizens, Experts, and the Environment: The Politics of Local Knowledge*, Durham, NC: Duke University Press.

Fishkin, J.S. (1997) *The Voice of the People*, New Haven: Yale University Press.

Fishkin, J.S. and Luskin, R.C. (2000) 'The Quest for Deliberative Democracy', in Saward, M. (ed.), *Democratic Innovation: Deliberation, Representation and Association*, London: Routledge.

Forester, J. (1992) 'Envisioning the Politics of Public-Sector Dispute Resolution', *Studies in Law, Politics and Society*, 12: 247–86.

Furrow, D. (1995) *Against Theory*, London: Routledge.

Gargarella, R. (1998) 'Full Representation, Deliberation, and Impartiality', in Elster, J. (ed.), *Deliberative Democracy*, Cambridge: Cambridge University Press.

Georgescu-Roegen, N. (1971) *The Entropy Law and the Economic Process*, Cambridge, MA: Harvard University Press.

Goodin, R.E. (1992) *Green Political Theory*, Cambridge: Polity.

Goodin, R. (1995) *Utilitarianism as a Public Philosophy*, Cambridge University Press.

Goodin, R. E. (1996) 'Enfranchising the Earth and its Alternatives', *Political Studies*, 44: 835–49.

Goodwin, B. (1992) *Justice by Lottery*, Chicago: University of Chicago Press.

Gouldson, A. and Murphy, J. (1997) 'Ecological Modernisation and Restructuring Industrial Economies', in Jacobs, M. (ed.), *Greening the Millennium*, Oxford: Blackwell.

Gray, J. (1995) *Berlin*, London: HarperCollins.

Gray, J. (2000) 'Where Pluralists and Liberals Part Company', in Baghramin, M. and Ingram, A. (eds), *Pluralism: The Philosophy and Politics of Diversity*, London: Routledge.

Grove-White, R. and O'Donovan, O. (1996) 'An Alternative Approach', in Attfield, R. and Dell, K. (eds), *Values, Conflict and the Environment* (second edition), Aldershot: Avebury.

Grundahl, J. (1995) 'The Danish Consensus Conference Model', in Joss, S. and Durant, J. (eds), *Public Participation in Science: The Role of Consensus Conferences in Europe*, London: Science Museum.

Gundersen, A.G. (1995) *The Environmental Promise of Democratic Deliberation*, Madison: University of Wisconsin Press.

Gutmann, A. (1996) 'Democracy, Philosophy, and Justification', in Benhabib, S. (ed.), *Democracy and Difference*, Princeton, NJ: Princeton University Press.

Gutmann, A. and Thompson, D. (1990) 'Moral Conflict and Political Consensus', *Ethics*, 101, 1: 64–88.

Gutmann, A. and Thompson, D. (1996) *Democracy and Disagreement*, Cambridge, MA, Belknap Press.

Habermas, J. (1971) *Knowledge and Human Interests*, Boston, MA: Beacon Press.

Habermas, J. (1975) *Legitimation Crisis*, Boston, MA: Beacon Press.

Habermas, J. (1981) *The Theory of Communicative Action*, Vol. 1, Cambridge: Polity.

Habermas, J. (1982) 'A Reply to my Critics', in Thompson, J. B. and Held, D. (eds), *Habermas: Critical Debates*, London: MacMillan.

Habermas, J. (1990) *Moral Consciousness and Communicative Action*, Cambridge, MA: MIT Press.

Habermas, J. (1993) *Justification and Application*, Cambridge: Polity.

Habermas, J. (1996a) 'Three Normative Models of Democracy', in Benhabib, S. (ed.), *Democracy and Difference*, Princeton: Princeton University Press.

Habermas, J. (1996b) *Between Facts and Norms*, Cambridge: Polity.

Hadden, S. (1995) 'Regulatory Negotiation as a Form of Public Participation', in Renn, O., Webler, T. and Wiedermann, P. (eds), *Fairness and Competence in Citizen Participation*, Dordrecht: Kluwer.

Hajer, M. (1995) *The Politics of Environmental Discourse: Ecological Modernisation and the Policy Process*, Oxford: Oxford University Press.

Hall, D. and Stewart, J. (1997) *Citizens' Juries in Local Government: Report from the LGMB on Pilot Projects*, Luton: LGMB.

Hampshire, S. (1983) *Morality and Conflict*, Oxford: Blackwell.

Hampshire, S. (1989) *Innocence and Experience*, Harmondsworth: Penguin.

Hare, R. M. (1981) *Moral Thinking*, Oxford: Clarendon Press.

Harsanyi, J.C. (1982) 'Morality and the Theory of Rational Behaviour', in Sen. A. and Williams, B. (eds), *Utilitarianism and Beyond*, Cambridge: Cambridge University Press.

Hayward, B. (1995) 'The Greening of Participatory Democracy: Reconsideration of Theory', *Environmental Politics*, 4, 4: 215–36.

Hayward, T. (1995) *Ecological Thought*, Cambridge: Polity.

Hayward, T. (1997) 'Anthropocentrism: A Misunderstood Problem', *Environmental Values*, 6, 1: 49–63.

Hayward, T. (1998) *Political Theory and Ecological Values*, Cambridge: Polity.

Hayward, T. (2000) 'Constitutional Environmental Rights: A Case for Political Analysis', *Political Studies*, 48, 3: 558–72.

Heidegger, M. (1962) *Being and Time*, Oxford: Blackwell.

Held, D. (1995) *Democracy and the Global Order*, Cambridge: Polity.

Hepburn, R.W. (1984) *Wonder and Other Essays*, Edinburgh: Edinburgh University Press.

Her Majesty's (HM) Treasury (1997) *Appraisal and Evaluation in Central Government: Treasury Guidance*, 2nd edn, London: HMSO.

Hill, T.E., Jr. (1994) 'Ideals of Human Excellence and Preserving the Natural Environment', in Gruen, L. and Jamieson, D. (eds), *Reflecting on Nature*, Oxford: Oxford University Press.

Hirst, P. (1994) *Associative Democracy*, Cambridge: Polity.

Hirst, P. (1997) *From Statism to Pluralism*, London: UCL Press.

Holland, A. (1994) 'Natural Capital', in Attfield, R. and Belsey, A. (eds), *Philosophy and the Natural Environment*, Cambridge: Cambridge University Press.

Hollis, M. (1994) *The Philosophy of Social Science*, Cambridge: Cambridge University Press.

Jacobs, M. (1991) *The Green Economy*, London: Pluto.

Jacobs, M. (1994) 'The Limits to Neoclassicism', in Redclift, M. and Benton, T. (eds), *Social Theory and the Global Environment*, London: Routledge.

Jacobs, M. (1995) 'Sustainable Development, Capital Substitution and Economic Humility: A Response to Beckerman', *Environmental Values*, 4: 57–68.

Jacobs, M. (1997) 'Environmental Valuation, Deliberative Democracy and Public Decision-Making Institutions', in Foster, J. (ed.), *Valuing Nature: Economics, Ethics and Environment*, London: Routledge.

Johnson, J. (1998) 'Arguing for Deliberation: Some Sceptical Comments', in Elster, J. (ed.), *Deliberative Democracy*, Cambridge: Cambridge University Press.

Jones-Lee, M. (1985) 'The Value of Safety: Results of a National Sample Survey', *Economic Journal*, 95: 49–72.

Jones-Lee, M. (1990) 'The Value of Transport Safety', *The Oxford Review of Economic Policy*, 6, 2: 39–60.

Joss, S. and Durant, J. (1995) 'The UK National Consensus Conference on Plant Biotechnology', *Public Understanding of Science*, 4: 195–204.

Kahnemann, D. and Knetsch, J. (1992) 'Valuing Public Goods: The Purchase of Moral Satisfaction', *Journal of Environmental Economics and Management*, 22: 57–70.

Kavka, G.S. and Warren, V. (1983) 'Political Representation for Future Generations', in Elliot, R. and Gare, A. (eds), *Environmental Philosophy*, Milton Keynes: Open University Press.

Keane, J. (1988) *Democracy and Civil Society*, London: Verso.

Keat, R. (1997) 'Values and Preferences in Neo-Classical Environmental Economics', in Foster, J. (ed.), *Valuing Nature: Economics, Ethics and Environment*, London: Routledge.

Kekes, J. (1993) *The Morality of Pluralism*, Princeton, NJ: Princeton University Press.

Klüver, L. (1995) 'Consensus Conferences at the Danish Board of Technology', in Joss, S. and Durant, J. (eds), *Public Participation in Science: The Role of Consensus Conferences in Europe*, London: Science Museum.

Knetsch, J. (1990) 'Environmental Policy Implications of Disparities between Willingness to Pay and Compensation Demanded Measures of Values', *Journal of Environmental Economics and Management*, 18: 227–37.

Knetsch, J. (1994) 'Environmental Valuation: Some Problems of Wrong Questions and Misleading Answers', *Environmental Values*, 3, 4: 351–68.

Kobach, K.W. (1994), 'Switzerland', in Butler, D. and Ranney, A. (eds), *Referendums Around the World*, Washington, DC: AEI Press.

Kuper, R. (1997) 'Deliberating Waste: The Hertfordshire Citizens' Jury', *Local Environment*, 2, 2: 139–53.

Linder, W. (1994) *Swiss Democracy*, New York: St. Martin's Press.

Lupia, A. and Johnston, R. (2001) 'Are Voters to Blame? Voter Competence and Elite Maneuvers in Referendums', in Mendelesohn, M. and Parkin, A. (eds), *Referendum Democracy: Citizens, Elites and Deliberation in Referendum Campaigns*, Basingstoke: Palgrave.

McCarthy, T. (1993) *Ideals and Illusions: On Reconstruction and Deconstruction in Contemporary Critical Theory*, Cambridge, MA: MIT Press.

McIver, S. (1997) *An Evaluation of the King's Fund Citizens' Juries Programme*, Birmingham: Health Services Management Centre.

Manin, B. (1987) 'On Legitimacy and Political Deliberation', *Political Theory*, 15, 3: 338–68.

Manin, B. (1997) *The Principles of Representative Government*, Cambridge: Cambridge University Press.

Mansbridge, J. (1983) *Beyond Adversarial Democracy*, Chicago: University of Chicago Press.

Mansbridge, J. (1995) 'A Deliberative Perspective on Neocorporatism', in Wright, E.O. (ed.), *Associations and Democracy*, London: Verso.

Mansbridge, J. (1996) 'Using Power/Fighting Power', in Benhabib, S. (ed.), *Democracy and Difference*, Princeton, NJ: Princeton University Press.

Mathews, F. (1991) *The Ecological Self*, London: Routledge.

Mayer, I., de Vries, J. and Geurts, J. (1995) 'An Evaluation of the Effects of Participation in a Consensus Conference', in Joss, S. and Durant. J. (eds), *Public Participation in Science*, London: Science Museum.

Mendelsohn, M. and Parkin, A. (2001) 'Introduction: Referendum Democracy', in Mendleson, M. and Parkin, A. (eds), *Referendum Democracy: Citizens, Elites and Deliberation in Referendum Campaigns*, Basingstoke: Palgrave.

Midgley, M. (1994) 'The End of Anthropocentrism?', in Attfield, R. and Belsey, A. (eds), *Philosophy and the Natural Environment*, Cambridge: Cambridge University Press.

Miller, D. (1992) 'Deliberative Democracy and Social Choice', *Political Studies Special Issue: Prospects for Democracy*, 40: 54–67.

Miller, D. (2002) 'Is Deliberative Democracy Unfair to Disadvantaged Groups?', in D'Entreves, M.P. (ed.), *Democracy as Public Deliberation: New Perspectives*, Manchester: Manchester University Press.

Mills, M. (1996) 'Green Democracy: The Search for an Ethical Solution', in Doherty, B. and de Geus, M. (eds), *Democracy and Green Political Thought*, London: Routledge.

Moon, J.D. (1995) 'Practical Discourse and Communicative Ethics', in White, S. (ed.), *The Cambridge Companion to Habermas*, Cambridge: Cambridge University Press.

Naess, A. (1973) 'The Shallow and the Deep, Long-Range Ecology Movements', *Inquiry*, 16: 95–100.

Naess, A. (1989) *Ecology, Community and Lifestyle*, Cambridge: Cambridge University Press.

Nagel, T. (1979a) 'What is it like to be a bat?', in *Mortal Questions*, Cambridge: Cambridge University Press.

Nagel, T. (1979b) 'The Fragmentation of Value', in *Mortal Questions*, Cambridge: Cambridge University Press.

Nash, C., Pearce, D. and Stanley, J. (1975) 'An Evaluation of Cost–benefit Analysis Criteria', *Scottish Journal of Political Economy*, 22, 2: 121–34.

National Center for Environmental Economics (NCEE) (2001) *Quality Economics for Today and Tomorrow*, Washington, DC: Environmental Protection Agency.

Nietzsche, F. (1994) *On The Genealogy of Morality*, Cambridge: Cambridge University Press.

Norton, B. (1986) 'On the Inherent Danger of Undervaluing Species', in Norton, B. (ed.), *The Preservation of Species: The Value of Biodiversity*, Princeton, NJ: Princeton University Press.

Norton, B. (1987) *Why Preserve Natural Variety?*, Princeton, NJ: Princeton University Press.

Offe, C. and Preuss, U.K. (1991) 'Democratic Institutions and Moral Resources' in Held, D. (ed.), *Political Theory Today*, Cambridge: Polity.

O'Neill, J. (1993) *Ecology, Policy and Politics: Human Well-Being and the Natural World*, London: Routledge.

O'Neill, J. (1997) 'Value Pluralism, Incommensurability and Institutions', in Foster, J. (ed.), *Valuing Nature: Economics, Ethics and Environment*, London: Routledge.

Organisation for Economic Co-operation and Development (OECD) (1989) *Environmental Policy Benefits: Monetary Valuation*, Paris: OECD.

O'Riordan, T. (1981) *Environmentalism*, London: Pion.

O'Riordan, T. and Jordan, A. (1995) 'The Precautionary Principle in Contemporary Environmental Politics', *Environmental Values*, 4: 191–212.

Ottmann, H. (1982) 'Cognitive Interests and Self-Reflection', in Thompson, J. B. and Held, D. (eds), *Habermas: Critical Debates*, London: MacMillan.

Owen, D. (1995) *Nietzsche, Modernity and Politics*, London: Sage.

Palmer, J. (ed.) (1999) *UK National Consensus Conference on Radioactive Waste: Final Report*, Cambridge: UKCEED.

Parry, G., Moyser, G. and Day, N. (1992) *Political Participation and Democracy in Britain*, Cambridge: Cambridge University Press.

Passmore, J. (1980) *Man's Responsibility for Nature*, 2nd edn, London: Duckworth.

Pearce, D. (1998) 'Cost–benefit Analysis and Environmental Policy', *Oxford Review of Economic Policy*, 14, 4: 84–100.

Pearce, D. and Turner, R.K. (1990) *Economics of Natural Resources and the Environment*, London: Harvester.

Pearce, D., Markandya, A. and Barbier, E.B. (1989) *Blueprint for a Green Economy*, London: Earthscan.

Pearce, D.W. and Nash, C.A. (1981) *The Social Appraisal of Projects*, London: Macmillan.

Perczynski, P. (2000) 'Active Citizenship and Associative Democracy, in Saward, M. (ed.), *Democratic Innovation: Deliberation, Representation and Association*, London: Routledge.

Phillips, A. (1995) *The Politics of Presence*, Oxford: Oxford University Press.

Pitkin, H. (1967) *The Concept of Representation*, Berkeley: University of California Press.

Plant, R. (1991) *Modern Political Thought*, Blackwell: Oxford.

Purdue, D. (1996) 'Contested Expertise: Plant Biotechnology and Social Movements', *Science as Culture*, 5, 4: 526–45.

Ratushinskaya, I. (1986) *No I am not Afraid*, Newcastle: Bloodaxe.

Rawls, J. (1993) *Political Liberalism*, New York: Columbia University Press.

Raz, J. (1986) *The Morality of Freedom*, Oxford: Oxford University Press.

Raz, J. and Griffin, J. (1991) 'Mixing Values', *Proceedings of the Aristotelian Society*, 65 (suppl.): 83–118.

Regan, T. (1988) *The Case for Animal Rights*, London: Routledge.

Renn, O., Webler, T. and Wiedemann, P. (1995) 'The Pursuit of Fair and Competent Citizen Participation', in Renn, O., Webler, T. and Wiedermann, P. (eds), *Fairness and Competence in Citizen Participation*, Dordrecht: Kluwer.

Rolston, H. (1983) 'Are Values in Nature Subjective or Objective?', in Elliot, R. and Gare, A. (eds), *Environmental Philosophy*, Milton Keynes: Open University Press.

Rorty, R. (1980) *Philosophy and the Mirror of Nature*, Oxford: Blackwell.

Rosenblum, N. (1998) *Membership and Morals*, Princeton, NJ: Princeton University Press.

Roßteutscher, S. (2000) 'Associative Democracy – Fashionable Slogan or Constructive Innovation', in Saward, M. (ed.), *Democratic Innovation: Deliberation, Representation and Association*, London: Routledge.

Routley, R. and Routley, V. (1995) 'Against the Inevitability of Human Chauvinism', in Elliot, R. (ed.), *Environmental Ethics*, Oxford: Oxford University Press.

RCEP (Royal Commission on Environmental Pollution) (1998) *Setting Environmental Standards* (Twenty-first Report), London: HMSO.

Sagoff, M. (1988) 'Some Problems with Environmental Ethics', *Environmental Ethics*, 10: 55–74.

Sale, K. (1985) *Dwellers in the Land: The Bioregional Vision*, San Francisco: Sierra Club.

Sanders, L.M. (1997) 'Against Deliberation', *Political Theory*, 25, 3: 347–76.

Saward, M. (1993) 'Green Democracy?', in Dobson, A. and Lucardie, P. (eds), *The Politics of Nature: Explorations in Green Political Theory*, London: Routledge.

Saward, M. (1996) 'Must Democrats be Environmentalists?', in Doherty, B. and de Geus, M. (eds), *Democracy and Green Political Thought*, London: Routledge.

Saward, M. (1998a) *Terms of Democracy*, Cambridge: Polity.

Saward, M. (1998b) 'Green State/Democratic State', *Contemporary Politics*, 4, 4: 345–56.

Saward, M. (2000a) 'Less Than Meets the Eye: Democratic Legitimacy and Deliberative Theory', in Saward, M. (ed.), *Democratic Innovation: Deliberation, Representation and Association*, London: Routledge.

Saward, M. (2000b) 'Direct and Deliberative Democracy', paper presented at the ECPR Joint Sessions, Copenhagen, http://www.essex.ac.uk/ecpr/jointsessions/Copenhagen/papers/ws20/saward.pdf.

Schlosberg, D. (1999) *Environmental Justice and the New Pluralism*, Oxford: Oxford University Press.

Seel, B., Patterson, M. and Doherty, B. (eds) (2000) *Direct Action in British Environmentalism*, London: Routledge.

Seiler, H. (1995) 'Review of "Planning Cells": Problems of Legitimation', in Renn, O., Webler, T. and Wiedermann, P. (eds), *Fairness and Competence in Citizen Participation*, Dordrecht: Kluwer.

Sen, A. (1977) 'Rational Fools', *Philosophy and Public Affairs*, 6: 317–44.

Sen, A. (1987) *On Ethics and Economics*, Oxford: Blackwell.

Smith, G. (2000) 'Towards Deliberative Institutions', in Saward, M. (ed.), *Democratic Innovation: Deliberation, Representation and Association*, London: Routledge.

Smith, G. (2001) 'Taking Deliberation Seriously: Institutional Design and Green Politics', *Environmental Politics*, 10, 3: 72–93.

Smith, G. and Wales, C. (1999) 'The Theory and Practice of Citizens' Juries', *Policy and Politics*, 27: 295–308.

Smith, G. and Wales, C. (2000) 'Citizens' Juries and Deliberative Democracy', *Political Studies*, 48, 1: 51–65.

Soper, K. (1995) *What is Nature?*, Oxford: Blackwell.

Squires, J. (1999) *Gender in Political Theory*, Cambridge: Polity.

Squires, J. (2000) 'Group Representation, Deliberation and the Displacement of Dichotomies', in Saward, M. (ed.), *Democratic Innovation: Deliberation, Representation and Association*, London: Routledge.

Squires, J. (2002) 'Deliberation and Decision-Making: Discontinuity in the Two-Track Model', in D'Entreves, M. P. (ed.), *Democracy as Public Deliberation: New Perspectives*, Manchester: Manchester University Press.

Standing Advisory Committee on Trunk Road Assessment (SACTRA) (1992) *Assessment of the Environmental Impact of Trunk Roads*, London: HMSO.

Stewart, J., Kendall, E. and Coote, A. (eds) (1994) *Citizens' Juries*, London: Institute of Public Policy Research.

Stone, C. (1987) *Earth and Other Ethics: The Case For Moral Pluralism*, New York: Harper and Row.

Stone, C. (1988) 'Moral Pluralism and the Course of Environmental Ethics', *Environmental Ethics*, 10: 139–54.

Sugden, R. and Williams, A. (1978) *The Principles of Practical Cost–Benefit analysis*, Oxford: Oxford University Press.

Sunstein, C.R. (1991) 'Preferences and Politics', *Philosophy and Public Affairs*, 20, 3–34.

Sunstein, C.R. (2002) 'The Law of Group Polarisation', *The Journal of Political Philosophy*, 10, 2: 175–95.

Susskind, L. and Cruikshank, J. (1987) *Breaking the Impasse*, New York: Basic Books.

Susskind, L. and Ozawa, C. (1985), 'Mediating Public Disputes: Obstacles and Possibilities', *Journal of Social Issues*, 41, 2: 145–59.

Taylor, B. P. (1996) 'Democracy and Environmental Ethics', in Lafferty, W. and Meadowcroft, J. (eds), *Democracy and the Environment*: Cheltenham, Edward Elgar.

Taylor, C. (1989) *Sources of the Self*, Cambridge: Cambridge University Press.

Taylor, C. (1992) *The Ethics of Authenticity*, Cambridge, MA: Harvard University Press.

Taylor, P. (1986) *Respect for Nature*, Princeton, NJ: Princeton University Press.

Thompson, J. (1983) 'Preservation of Wilderness and the Good Life' in Elliot, R. and Gare, A. (eds), *Environmental Philosophy*, Milton Keynes: Open University Press.

Thompson, J. (1990) 'A Refutation of Environmental Ethics', *Environmental Ethics*, 12, 2: 147–60.

Torgerson, D. (1999) *The Promise of Green Politics*, Durham and London: Dukes University Press.

Turner, R.K., Pearce, D. and Bateman, I. (1994) *Environmental Economics*, London: Harvester Wheatsheaf.

UKNCC (UK National Consensus Conference) (1994) *Lay Panel Preliminary Report*, London: Science Museum.

Vadnjal, D. and O'Connor, M. (1994) 'What is the Value of Rangitoto Island?', *Environmental Values*, 3, 4: 369–80.

Vogel, S. (1996) *Against Nature: The Concept of Nature in Critical Theory*, New York: State University of New York Press.

Waldron, J. (1999) *The Dignity of Legislation*, Cambridge: Cambridge University Press.

Wall, D. (1999) *Earth First! and the Anti-Roads Movement*, London: Routledge.

Warren, M. (1995) 'The Self in Discursive Democracy', in White, S. (ed.), *The Cambridge Companion to Habermas*, Cambridge: Cambridge University Press.

Warren, M. (1996a) 'What Should We Expect from More Democracy?', *Political Theory*, 24, 2: 241–70.

Warren, M. (1996b) 'Deliberative Democracy and Authority', *American Political Science Review*, 90, 1: 46–60.

Warren, M. (1998) 'What Should Democrats Expect of Associations?', paper presented at the Annual Meeting of the American Political Science Association, Boston, 3–6 September.

Weale, A. (1992) *The New Politics of Pollution*, Manchester University Press.

Westra, L. (1989) 'Ecology and Animals: Is There a Joint Ethic of Respect?', *Environmental Ethics*, 11: 215–30.

Whitebook, J. (1979) 'The Problem of Nature in Habermas', *Telos*, 40: 41–69.

Williams, B. (1973a) *Problems of the Self*, Cambridge: Cambridge University Press.

Williams, B. (1973b) 'A Critique of Utilitarianism', in Smart, J. and Williams, B. (eds), *Utilitarianism: For and Against*, Cambridge: Cambridge University Press.

Williams, B. (1981) *Moral Luck*, Cambridge: Cambridge University Press.

Williams, B. (1985) *Ethics and the Limits of Philosophy*, Cambridge, MA: Harvard University Press.

Williams, B. (1995) *Making Sense of Humanity and other philosophical papers 1982–1993*, Cambridge: Cambridge University Press.

Williams, B. (1996) 'Truth in Ethics', in Hooker, B. (ed.), *Truth in Ethics*, Oxford: Blackwell.

Williams, M. (2000) 'The Uneasy Alliance of Group Representation and Deliberative Democracy', in Kymlica, W. and Norman, W. (eds), *Citizenship in Diverse Societies*, Oxford: Oxford University Press.

Wilson, E.O. (1992) *The Diversity of Life*, London: Penguin.

Winpenny, J.T . (1991) *Values for the Environment: A Guide to Economic Appraisal*, London: HMSO.

Wissenburg, M. (1998) *Green Liberalism: The Free and Green Society*, London: UCL Press.

Witoszek, N. and Brennan, A. (1999) *Philosophical Dialogues: Arne Naess and the Progress of Ecophilosophy*, Lanham: Rowman and Littlefield.

Wolf, S. (1992) 'Two Levels of Pluralism', *Ethics*, 102, 3: 785–98.

World Commission on Environment and Development (WCED) (1987) *Our Common Future*, Oxford: Oxford University Press.

Wynne, B. (1996) 'May the Sheep Safely Graze? A Reflexive View of the Expert-Lay Knowledge Divide', in Lash, S., Szerszynski, B. and Wynne, B. (eds), *Risk, Environment and Modernity: Towards a New Ecology*, London: Sage.

Young, I.M. (1990a) 'The Ideal of Community and the Politics of Difference', in Nicholson, L. (ed.), *Feminism/Postmodernism*, London: Routledge.

Young, I.M. (1990b) *Justice and the Politics of Difference*, Princeton, NJ: Princeton University Press.

Young, I.M. (1995) 'Social Groups in Associative Democracy', in Wright, E. O. (ed.), *Associations and Democracy*, London: Verso.

Young, I. M. (1996) 'Communication and the Other: Beyond Deliberative Democracy', in Benhabib, S. (ed.), *Democracy and Difference*, Princeton, NJ: Princeton University Press.

Young, I.M. (2000) *Inclusion and Democracy*, Oxford: Oxford University Press.

Index